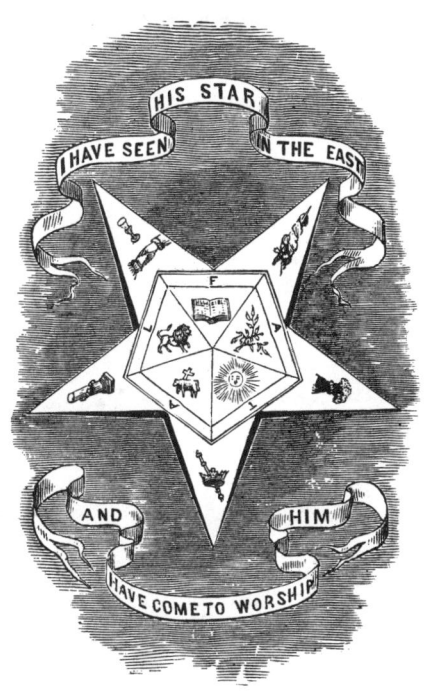

AND altogether blest
   Are those who know the Lord:
The grave will kindly yield its guest
   To his resistless word.

Courteously yours
Robt. Macoy

ADOPTIVE RITE RITUAL

A BOOK OF INSTRUCTION

in the Organization, Government
and Ceremonies

OF

CHAPTERS

OF THE ORDER OF THE

EASTERN STAR

TOGETHER WITH

THE QUEEN OF THE SOUTH

ARRANGED BY

ROBERT MACOY

PAST GRAND SECRETARY OF THE SUPREME GRAND
CHAPTER

19th Reprinting

Macoy Publishing & Masonic Supply Co., Inc.

Richmond, Virginia

Entered, according to Act of Congress, in the year 1868,
By the Masonic Publishing and Manufacturing Company,
In the Clerk's office of the District court of the United States
for the Southern District of New York.

Copyright, by J.G. Barker, 1897.

Copyright, 1928, 1952, Copyright Renewed 1980 by
Macoy Publishing & Masonic Supply Co., Inc.

ISBN-0-88053-300-5

Printed in the United States of America

PREFACE

Having been engaged for a number of years in the dissemination of the beautiful Order of the Eastern Star, and believing that the system is fast becoming deeply rooted in the affections of the Craft and their female relatives; and that the time is not far distant when this system of the Adoptive Rite will receive official recognition, and meet with general acceptance, even where it is now neglected or proscribed, has been the impelling influence for offering this volume upon the plan here suggested.

The want of some systematic organization has been the leading cause in retarding its general usefulness. It may be set down as an axiom, that no degree, however remotely connected with any institution, can take a high place among us unless it possess a well-conceived and philosophic basis of ceremonial, symbolism and constitutional regulation. Without these it is subject to constant changes from a multiplicity of minds, which tend to destroy its universality and give its opponents just grounds for their cavillings. The history of all the Masonic degrees (above the first three) proves this. The degrees of the Chapter, Council and

Commandery were never prized until in the last generation they were thus wrought out, framed together and perfectly systematized. Their opponents have now become their warmest advocates, and they stand upon an immutable foundation.

Believing that there are equal grounds of stability in the system of the Eastern Star, the present Ritual is presented. In this pleasant labor I have had the counsel of the highest lights of the Adoptive System. Dr. Morris, whose labors in connection with this subject are well known, has given his unqualified approbation of the present plan. I have every reason to believe that in the preparation of this work nothing has been left undone that will conduce to the permanency, prosperity and extended usefulness of the Order of the Eastern Star.

ROBT. MACOY

PUBLISHERS' FOREWORD

THIS edition in no way deviates from the true ritual as compiled by the venerable Robert Macoy. Nor will the previous editions be obsolete.

Sketchy instructions which have appeared in the earlier printings have been put into dialogue and diagrams for winding the labyrinth have been added. Some very important and much needed additions have been made: TRUSTEES, MARSHAL, MUSICIAN, and FLAG BEARERS have been included in the list of officers, together with their duties in the ritualistic work, opening and installation ceremonies. Since World War I it has become proper for all gatherings, fraternal or otherwise, to display the American Flag at meetings. Many Grand Chapters authorize the Christian Flag and the Eastern Star Flag as well. It is, therefore, fitting that these officers should be given rightful recognition along with the other officers and we believe these additions will be highly acceptable. And those Grand Chapters authorizing an ASSOCIATE PATRON and a CHAPLAIN will find the work and duties for these optional officers also included. The material on optional officers has been set in italics so that no confusion will arise and these sections may be omitted if such officers are not authorized by your Grand Chapter.

The sections on BALLOTING, MEMBERSHIP, ORGANIZING A SUBORDINATE CHAPTER, CHAPTER MEETINGS, etc., will, we trust, be welcome additions to the book. The ADMINISTRATIVE DEGREE, while not changed, has been made to include the Worthy Patron as well as the Worthy Matron. Popular usage of the degree for both has prompted this addition, but may be omitted if desired.

Illustrations of all officers' jewels and regalia have been included, but we have been most careful to retain all the original early illustrations which greatly enhance the book.

Finally, the material has been so organized and arranged that quick reference to any section is an easy matter by consulting the Contents Page.

It is the earnest hope of the Publishers that the arrangement of this edition will help to still further aid in the spread of enlightenment of the Order of the Eastern Star and contribute to a more dignified and beautiful rendition of the work.

THE PUBLISHERS

New York, August, 1952

CONTENTS

	Page
Preface	3
Publishers' Foreword	5
Contents	7
Historical Sketch	9
The Landmarks	13
Objects and Purposes of the Rite	15
The Degrees of the Order of the Eastern Star	16
Membership	18
Petition for a Lady	19
Petition from a Master Mason	20
Petition for Affiliation	21
Certificate of Withdrawal (Dimit)	22
Certificate for one dropped from the roll at own request	23
Forfeiture of Membership	23
Restoration of Membership	23
Original Powers, Authority, and Duties of Subordinate Chapters	24
Officers and Their Stations	25
Elective	27
Appointive	27
Optional	27
Jewels and Regalia	28
Chapter Paraphernalia	48
Chapter Meetings	50
Quorum	50
Use of the Gavel	51

CONTENTS

Raps	51
Admission of Visitors	51
OPENING CEREMONIES	53
With Flag Bearers	71
ORDER OF BUSINESS	75
CLOSING CEREMONIES	76
With Retiring of Flag(s)	80
BALLOTING	82
INITIATION	86
INITIATION OF A MASTER MASON	131
AFFILIATION CEREMONY	138
QUEEN OF THE SOUTH	140
MATRONS' AND PATRONS' ADMINISTRATIVE DEGREE	166
Form of Certificate	182
ELECTION OF OFFICERS	183
INSTALLATION OF OFFICERS OF A SUBORDINATE CHAPTER	185
INSTALLATION OF THE OFFICERS OF A GRAND CHAPTER	212
PARLIAMENTARY LAW ADAPTED TO A CHAPTER	226
PETITION TO ORGANIZE A SUBORDINATE CHAPTER	228
CONSTITUTING AND INAUGURATING A CHAPTER	230
DEDICATION OF EASTERN STAR HALL	244
CHAPTER OF SORROW	262
BURIAL SERVICE	279
THE PENTAGRAM	293

THE ADOPTIVE RITE

HISTORICAL SKETCH

SECRET societies, imitating Freemasonry, for the admission of females as members, were first organized in France about the year 1730, and still exist there and in other parts of Europe as a distinct Rite.

By the term *Adoptive Rite* is implied that system of forms, ceremonies, and explanatory lectures which is communicated to certain classes of ladies, who, from their relationship by blood or marriage to Master Masons in good standing, are entitled to the respect and attention of the entire Fraternity.

These ladies are said to have been *adopted* into the Masonic communion, because the system of forms, ceremonies, and lectures above referred to enabled them to express their wishes, and give satisfactory evidence of their claims, in a manner that no stranger to the Masonic family could.

To the organizations thus established for the initiation of females the French have given the name of "Adoptive Masonry," *Maconnerie d' Adoption,* and the Lodges are called *Loges d' Adoption,* or "Adoptive Lodges," because every lodge of females was obliged to be adopted by, and under the guardianship of, some regular Masonic lodge.

One of the first of these societies was the "Order of Perfect Happiness," for so we may be permitted to translate the name of "Felicitares," which they adopted. This society assumed a nautical character in its emblems and its vocabulary. It was divided into the four degrees of "Cabin-Boy," "Master," "Commodore," and "Vice-Admiral." What little information we have been enabled to obtain from a very brief notice of its ritual leads us to believe that it was not of a character to merit countenance. It did not long retain its existence, for two years after its formation it gave place to the "Knights and Heroines of the Anchor," which was, however, but a refinement of the original society, and preserved its formula of initiation and nearly all its ceremonies.

In 1747 a new society was instituted called "L'Order des Fendeurs," or the Order of Wood-cutters. It borrowed its principal ceremonies from the society of the Carbonari, or Coal-burners, which had been previously established in Italy. The place of meeting of the Wood-cutters was called the "wood-yard," and was supposed to represent a forest; the presiding officer was called "Father Master," and the male and female members were styled "Cousins." This society became at once exceedingly popular, and the most distinguished ladies and gentlemen of France united themselves to it. It was, consequently, the cause of the institution of many similar societies, such as the Order of the Hatchet, of Fidelity, etc.

In consequence of the increasing popularity of the numerous secret associations, which in their external characters and mysterious rites attempted an imitation of Freemasonry, differing, however, from that institution, of which they were, perhaps, the rivals for public favor, by the admission of female members, the Grand Orient of France, in 1774, established a new rite, called the "Rite of Adoption," which was placed under the control of the Grand Orient. Rules and regulations were provided for the government of these Lodges of Adoption, one of which was that no men should be permitted to attend them except regular Freemasons, and that each lodge should be placed under the charge and held under the sanction and warrant, of some regularly constituted Masonic lodge, whose Master, or, in his absence, his Deputy, should be the presiding officer, assisted by a female President or Mistress.

Under these regulations a Lodge of Adoption was opened at Paris in 1775, under the patronage of the Lodge of St. Anthony, in which the Duchess of Bourbon presided and was installed as Grand Mistress of the Adoptive Rite. The doctrines inculcated in this order were intended to remind the members of their especial duties in this world, and the words addressed by the Grand Mistress to the aspirant revealed the nature of the trials and of the instruction which awaited her in the successive degrees into which she sought to be initiated. The aspirant was warned against entering the society through a mere feeling of curiosity, and was informed that the order was destined to render human society as perfect as possible. She was taught to love justice and charity, to be free from prejudice and bigotry, to hate artifice and falsehood, and, by her virtue, to gain the universal esteem and friendship of her Brothers and Sisters.

The candidate took the following oath: "In the presence of the Grand Architect of the Universe, I swear faithfully to keep the secrets entrusted to me; if I betray them may I be forever dishonored and despised; and in order that I may have strength to keep my promise, may a spark of divine light illumine and protect my heart, and lead me in the paths of virtue." This promise was sealed with three kisses which the Grand Mistress gave her— the kiss of peace on the forehead, the kiss of faith on the right cheek, and the kiss of friendship on the left cheek.

Many systems of the Adoptive Rite have, from time to time, been introduced into the United States, with varied success, but none of which seemed to possess the elements of permanency, until the introduction of the Order of the EASTERN STAR, which was established in this country during the year 1778. The success of this Order, as now conducted, corresponds in its usefulness with the extent of similar institutions.

THE LANDMARKS

1. The Eastern Star is the basis of the Five Degrees of the Adoptive Rite; the name and character of the Rite are unchangeable.

2. Its lessons are Scriptural; its teachings are moral; and its purposes are beneficent.

3. Its obligations are based upon the honor of the female sex who obtain its ceremonies, and are framed upon the principle that whatever benefits are due by the Masonic Fraternity *to* the wives, widows, daughters and sisters of Masons, corresponding benefits are due *from* them to the Brotherhood.

4. Each candidate shall declare a belief in the existence of a Supreme Being, who will, sooner or later, punish the willful violation of a solemn pledge.

5. The modes of recognition, which are the peculiar secrets of the Rite, cannot, without de-

stroying the foundation of the system, be changed.

6. A covenant of secrecy voluntarily assumed is perpetual; from the force of such obligation there is no possibility of release.

7. The control of the Rite lies in a central head, styled the Supreme Council or Grand Chapter of the Adoptive Rite, or in the prerogatives of the Supreme Grand Patron, when the Supreme Grand Chapter in not in session.

8. The ballot for candidates for membership must be unanimous, and is to be kept inviolably secret.

9. It is the right of every Chapter to be the judge of who shall be admitted to its membership, and to select its own officers, but in no case can the ceremonies of the Order be conferred unless a Master Mason in good standing in the Masonic Fraternity presides.

10. Every member is amenable to the laws and regulations of the Order, and may be tried for offenses, though he or she may permanently or temporarily reside within the jurisdiction of another Chapter.

11. It is the right of every member to appeal from the decision of a Subordinate Chapter to the Supreme Council or Grand Chapter, or to the Supreme or Grand Patron.

12. It is the prerogative of the Supreme, or Grand Patron to preside over every assembly of the

Rite wherever he may visit, and to grant Dispensations for the formation of new Chapters.

13. Every Chapter has the right to dispense the light of the Adoptive Rite and to administer its own private affairs.

14. Every Chapter should elect and install its officers annually.

15. It is the right of every member to visit and sit in every regular Chapter, except when such visitor is likely to disturb the harmony or interrupt the progress of the Chapter he or she proposes to visit.

OBJECTS AND PURPOSES OF THE RITE

The objects and purposes are the cultivation of charitable and fraternal practices that we may comfort, protect and aid each other in our journey through the labyrinth of human life; for a more extended diffusion of the principles of morality and friendship by established and significant emblems; for inciting the influence of females towards the purposes of the Masonic institution; for increasing social enjoyment by the aid of the Masonic tie; for ameliorating the condition of the destitute widow and the helpless orphan; and for affording increased facilities in relieving distressed female travelers. For these purposes the Adoptive Rite has been framed.

The wives, mothers, widows, sisters and daughters of Masons cannot, from the immutable laws of the Order, be permitted to share in the grand mysteries of Freemasonry; but there is no reason why there should not be a society for them, which may not merely enable them to make themselves known to Masons, and so to obtain assistance and protection, but by means of which, acting in concert through the tie of association and mutual obligation, they may cooperate in the great labors of Masonry, by assisting in, and in some respects directing, the charities, and toiling in the cause of human progress.

To secure successful results to a purpose so laudable it is necessary that its votaries should apply its rules in a rigid sense; carefully maintain its landmarks; affiliate into its bonds only those who are well calculated by temperament and principle to understand and appreciate its beauties and work out patiently and untiringly its grand designs.

THE DEGREES OF THE ORDER OF THE EASTERN STAR

The Five Degrees of the Order of the Eastern Star are founded on the Holy Scriptures. Five worthy and notable female characters, illustrating as many moral virtues, have been selected and adopted. These are:

1. ADAH, JEPHTHAH'S DAUGHTER, illustrating *integrity, filial devotion and respect to the binding force of a vow.*

2. RUTH, illustrating *industry, loyalty and devotion to religious principles.*

3. ESTHER, illustrating *justice, courage and fidelity to kindred and friends.*

4. MARTHA, illustrating *undeviating faith in the hour of trial and the immortality of the soul.*

5. ELECTA, illustrating *fervency, love, generosity and patience and submission under wrongs.*

These virtues have nowhere in history more brilliant exemplars than in the five characters illustrated in the lectures of the Order of the Eastern Star.

The honorable and exalted purposes had in view in its dissemination can have no opposition worthy the name. Its effects in winning to the advocacy of charity the virtuous, intelligent and influential female members of our families are truly encouraging, and stimulate its friends to persevere in a general promulgation of the system.

According to the tenets of the Order of the Eastern Star, the Adoptive Rite stands a bright monument to female secrecy and fidelity, and proves how wrong all those are who fancy a woman is not to be trusted. There is not in the whole of the ceremonies of this Rite a single point with which the most ascetic moralist could find fault.

As the adoptive priviliges of the lady entirely depend upon the good standing and affiliation of the Brother through whom she is introduced, this system will be a strong inducement, it is believed, to keep a Brother, otherwise inclined to err, within the bounds of morality.

MEMBERSHIP

Membership in the Order of the Eastern Star is by unanimous election or by affiliation.

The body when assembled is called a "Chapter of the Order of the Eastern Star," which shall be composed of males and females, and must consist of not less than seven ladies who are the wives, mothers, widows, sisters, or daughters of Master Masons in good standing.

The benefits of this Rite are primarily for women, the extent of which will depend upon the spirit with which they enter into and conduct their affairs in the Rite.

The female members of this Rite are called *Sisters;* male members, *Brothers*.

The lawful recipients of the Adoptive Rite are such worthy females—being wives, mothers, widows, daughters, or sisters of affiliated Master Masons—as may be regularly proposed by one and recommended by another member of the Chapter, and unanimously elected by the members at a stated meeting of the Chapter. The petition must in all cases be referred to a committee of three members for investigation, and lay over at least one regular meeting before ballot. The sister or daughter of a Mason, if unmarried, must have attained the age of eighteen years to be eligible for initiation or membership.

Mastor Masons, affiliated in regular Lodges, may be proposed by one or more members of the Chapter, and must be unanimously elected.

The Brother, if elected, will be required to pledge his honor as a Master Mason, in open Chapter, to conform to the rules and regulations of the Order.

FORM OF PETITION FOR MEMBERSHIP FOR A LADY
.....................19

*To the Worthy Matron, Officers and Members of.....
Chapter, No..., of the Order of the Eastern Star:*
Your petitioner, the (*wife, mother, widow, sister, or daughter*) of Bro......., of...... Lodge, No......., located at ......, State of....., solicits the light and privileges of the Order of the Eastern Star in your Chapter.

If the prayer of her petition is granted, she pledges her honor that she will, in all respects, conform to the legal requirements of your Chapter, and be subject to

the rules and regulations of the Grand Chapter in this State.
Do you believe in a Supreme Being?..............
Name in full....................................
Born at...
Residence ....
Is this application of your own free will?............
Have you ever presented a petition to, or been rejected by any Chapter, O. E. S., and if so, when, and what Chapter?
....
Signature .... Address ....
Proposed by ....
References: { .... Address ....
{ .... Address ....
{ .... Address ....
The proposition fee, $........ must accompany this application.

FORM OF PETITION FROM A MASTER MASON

..................19

To the Worthy Matron, Officers and Members of ...... Chapter, No. ......, of the Order of the Eastern Star:

Your petitioner, a Master Mason, and a member in good standing in .... Lodge, No. ...., held at ......, solicits the light and knowledge of the Eastern Star in your Chapter.

If the prayer of his petition is granted, he pledges his honor as a Master Mason, that he will, in all respects, conform to the legal requirements of your Chapter, and

MEMBERSHIP 21

be subject to the constitutional rules and regulations of
the Grand Chapter in this State.

Signature ....Address..............
Proposed by ....Address..............

FORM OF PETITION FOR AFFILIATION

A sister or a brother demitted from one Chapter,
and wishing to affiliate with another, will use the
following form of petition:

....................19
To the Worthy Matron, Officers and Members of ......
   Chapter, No. ......, of the Order of the Eastern
   Star:

The undersigned, late a member of ...... Chapter,
No. ...., as certified by the accompanying certificate of
withdrawal, solicits affiliation with your Chapter.

If this petition is granted, she (he) pledges her honor
(his honor as a Mason) to conform, in all respects, to the
legal requirements of your Chapter.

(Signed,)

Proposed by ....Address..............
Recommended by ....Address..............

The petition must be accompanied by a dimit or
certificate of withdrawal from the last Chapter of
which the petitioner was a member, which may be
obtained by a majority vote, and is in the following
form:

FORM OF CERTIFICATE OF WITHDRAWAL (DIMIT)

"We have seen his star in the East,
And are come to worship him."

To all Enlightened Members of the Order of the Eastern Star, wherever dispersed, this Certificate of Withdrawal witnesseth:

This is to certify that Sister (*Brother*) ...., whose name appears on the margin of this DIMIT, was initiated into the light of the Adoptive Rite (*or affiliated*) in ...... Chapter No. ...., located at ...., on the .. day of ...., 19...

That during her (*his*) connection with us, she (*he*) has in all respects conformed to the legal requirements of this Chapter, and the constitutional rules and regulations of the Supreme Grand Chapter.

That in her (*his*) withdrawal, she (*he*) bears with her (*him*) the love and esteem of the officers and members of this Chapter; and we affectionately commend her (*him*) to the friendship and protection of all enlightened members of the Order wherever in the journey of life she (*he*) may be found.

In Testimony Whereof, We have caused this DIMIT to be signed by the Worthy Matron and Worthy Patron, and the Seal of the Chapter attached, this .... day of ...., 19...

(SEAL)

........................Worthy Matron
........................Worthy Patron
Attest: .... Secretary

FORM OF CERTIFICATE FOR ONE DROPPED FROM THE ROLL AT OWN REQUEST

To Whom it may Concern, GREETING:

This is to certify that ...., a member of .... Chapter No. ...., located at ...., State of ...., having paid all her (*his*) indebtedness, was dropped from the roll of this Chapter on ...... day of ...., 19.., at her (*his*) own request.

Given under our hands and Seal of the Chapter at ...., this ...... day of ...., 19...
(SEAL)

........................Worthy Matron
........................Worthy Patron
Attest: .... Secretary

FORFEITURE OF MEMBERSHIP

The membership of a Brother is forfeited:

1. By suspension, expulsion, dimission, or withdrawal from the Masonic Lodge of which he was a member.

2. By suspension, expulsion, dimission, or withdrawal from membership in the Chapter.

Restoration by, or affiliation with, a Lodge will remove the first cause; restoration by the Chapter will remove the second.

The membership of a Sister is forfeited:

1. By absence from the sessions of the Chapter for two years without just cause.

2. By suspension, expulsion, dimission, or withdrawal from the Chapter.

3. By the suspension, expulsion, dimission, or withdrawal of the Brother through whom she was adopted upon her original petition.

Restoration by the Chapter will remove the first and second causes. Cause three may be removed if she can prove adoption through another Master Mason, affiliated and in good standing. The members of the Chapter are at liberty to substitute his name on the original petition.

ORIGINAL POWERS, AUTHORITY AND DUTIES OF SUBORDINATE CHAPTERS

The membership of a Subordinate Chapter have original powers and authority for action in the following matters:

1. In all matters of discipline involving inquiry into misconduct, and trial and punishment for the same. However, that in all cases, an appeal to the Supreme Grand Chapter or to the Most Eminent Grand Patron shall be allowed.

2. In all appropriations of the funds of the Chapter.

3. In the free choice and selection of its own officers and members.

4. In the disposition of its own property, except its Charter, books of record and accounts, and rituals. These, of right, belong to the Supreme Grand Chapter.

5. All Chapters under the jurisdiction of the Supreme Grand Chapter must make returns annually of its work showing the total number of members, the number initiated, affiliated, withdrawn, suspended, expelled or died, until a State Grand Chapter shall be organized, when that Grand Body will assume authority over all Subordinate Chapters within its jurisdiction and will be given the annual returns.

OFFICERS AND THEIR STATIONS

The number of officers comprising a complete Chapter will depend on: (1) authorization by the Grand Chapter of the State of part, or all, of the *optional* officers designated by †; (2) size of the Chapter. Small Chapters, or newly organized ones, may not have enough members for all the optional officers listed.

Nearly every Grand Chapter now requires that a Chapter have three Trustees as well as a Musician (Organist or Pianist) and a Marshal. In addition, several have found it wise to have an Associate Patron who can take over the duties of the Worthy Patron should the Patron, on occasion due to his vocation, find it a hardship to attend a meeting.

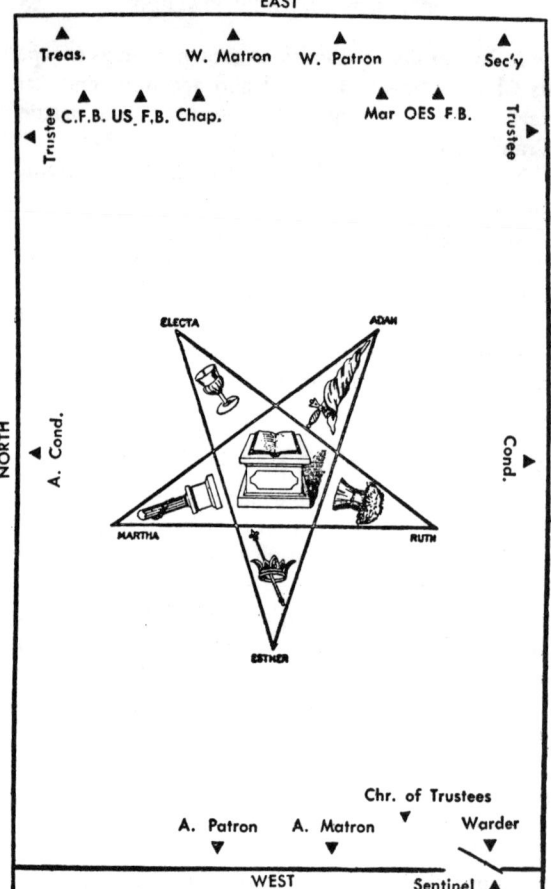

OFFICERS AND THEIR STATIONS

Every Chapter should, of course, display the American or National Flag and many display the Christian and Eastern Star Flags as well. Flag Bearers add greatly to the impressiveness of the ceremonies and it seems only fitting that recognition should be given to such officers.

Some Grand Chapters have authorized a Chaplain who is seated in front and to the right of the Matron, at the foot of the dais, and gives the prayers rather than the Patron.

Elective Officers are:

1. WORTHY MATRON, in the East.
2. WORTHY PATRON, in the East, to the left of the Matron.
3. ASSOCIATE MATRON, in the West.
† 4. ASSOCIATE PATRON, in the West, to the left of the A. M.
5. TREASURER, at the right of the Matron in the East.
6. SECRETARY, at the left of the Matron in the East.
7. CONDUCTRESS, in the South.
8. ASSOCIATE CONDUCTRESS, in the North.
† 9. CHAIRMAN OF THE TRUSTEES, to the right of the A. M. in the West.
† 10. TRUSTEE, near the Treasurer in the East.
† 11. TRUSTEE, near the Secretary in the East.

Appointive Officers are:

† 12. CHRISTIAN FLAG BEARER, to the left of and in front of the Treasurer.
† 13. U.S. FLAG BEARER, to the left of the Christian Flag Bearer.

- † 14. O.E.S. Flag Bearer, to the left and in front of the Patron.
- 15. Marshal, in front of the Patron and to the right of the O.E.S. Flag Bearer.
- † 16. Musician, at the organ or piano.
- 17. Warder, near the door inside the Chapter room.
- 18. Sentinel, at the door outside the Chapter room.
- 19. Adah, on the first, or Blue point, of the Star.
- 20. Ruth, on the second, or Yellow point, of the Star.
- 21. Esther, on the third, or White point, of the Star.
- 22. Martha, on the fourth, or Green point, of the Star.
- 23. Electa, on the fifth, or Red point, of the Star.
- † 24. Chaplain, in front and to the right of the Matron at the foot of the dais.

JEWELS AND REGALIA

The Officers will be distinguished by their jewels of yellow metal which may be suspended from a cord or ribbon worn around the neck, or from a short ribbon fastened to a bar pin top which may be pinned on the breast or sash.

Worthy Matron—Gavel within a Star.

Worthy Patron—Square and Compasses within a Star.

Associate Matron—Refulgent Sun within a Star.

Associate Patron—Rayed Star within a Star.

JEWELS AND REGALIA 29

(Taken from an early edition of *The Adoptive Rite*)

Treasurer—Crossed Keys within a Star.

Secretary—Crossed Pens within a Star.

Conductress—Scroll and Baton crossed within a Star.

Associate Conductress—Baton within a Star.

Trustees—Key within a Star.

Christian Flag Bearer—Christian Flag within a Star.

U.S. Flag Bearer—U.S. Flag within a Star.

O.E.S. Flag Bearer—O.E.S. Flag within a Star.

Marshal—Crossed Batons within a Star.

MUSICIAN—Lyre within a Star.
WARDER—Dove within a Star.
SENTINEL—Crossed Swords within a Star.
ADAH—Sword and Veil within a Triangle.
RUTH—Sheaf of Wheat within a Triangle.
ESTHER—Crown and Scepter within a Triangle.
MARTHA—Broken column within a Triangle.
ELECTA—Cup within a Triangle.
CHAPLAIN—Open Bible within a Star.

The appropriate COLORS are: BLUE for Adah, Jephthah's Daughter; YELLOW for Ruth; WHITE for Esther; GREEN for Martha; and RED for Electa. These five colors combined make up the official ribbon of the Rite.

A Sash, or Scarf, of the five colors, three or four inches wide, with a five-colored star on the shoulder and an emblematic five-colored star, or gold-colored rosette at the crossing, worn from the right shoulder to the left side, is the distinctive regalia of the Order for the officers.

It has become customary for the Worthy Matron and Associate Matron to wear distinctive sashes of royal purple velvet; the Five Star Points, sashes of their respective station color, and the remaining officers, sashes of the five colors combined, with exception of the Chaplain, who wears a white sash or stole. The Worthy Patron and Associate Patron may wear a five-colored ribbon collar or purple velvet collar, from which the jewel of office is sus-

JEWELS AND REGALIA 31

pended. The Patron may also wear a Patron's apron of purple velvet or one of five colors.

Members wear five-colored membership badges.

Past Matrons wear royal purple velvet sashes with embroidered vine work with crossed gavels and with the letters "P. M." and the years they served as Matron. Their jewel is the emblematic star with a gavel and may take the form of a jewel or a pin.

Member's Badge
(May be reversed for mourning purposes)

32　　　　ADOPTIVE RITE RITUAL

Past Matron's Sash

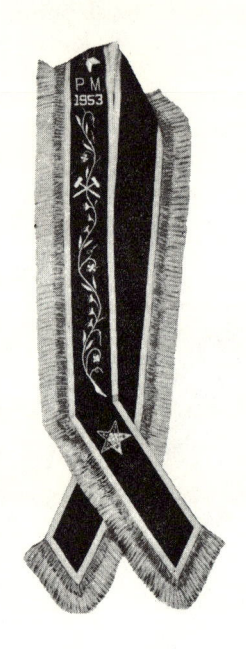

JEWELS AND REGALIA 33

Worthy Matron

34 ADOPTIVE RITE RITUAL

Worthy Patron

Associate Patron

Patron's Collar

JEWELS AND REGALIA 35

Patron's Aprons

ADOPTIVE RITE RITUAL

Associate Matron

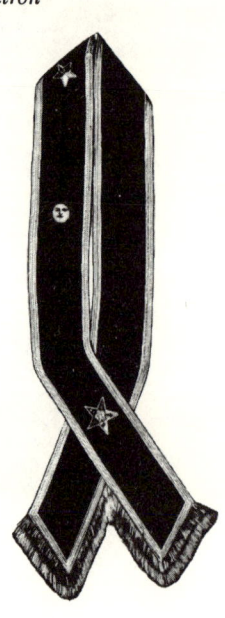

JEWELS AND REGALIA 37

Treasurer

Secretary

38　　　　　　ADOPTIVE RITE RITUAL

Conductress

Associate Conductress

JEWELS AND REGALIA 39

Marshal

Warder

The officers, whose jewels appear on this page, wear the five-colored sashes as shown for the Conductresses. However, if the Trustees are Past Matrons, they will wear their P.M. sashes in place of the five-colored ones.

Musician

Trustee

40 ADOPTIVE RITE RITUAL

U.S. Flag Bearer

O.E.S. Flag Bearer

The O.E.S. Flag Bearer wears a five-colored sash, such as shown on page 38.

JEWELS AND REGALIA 41

Christian Flag Bearer

Chaplain

ADOPTIVE RITE RITUAL

Sentinel

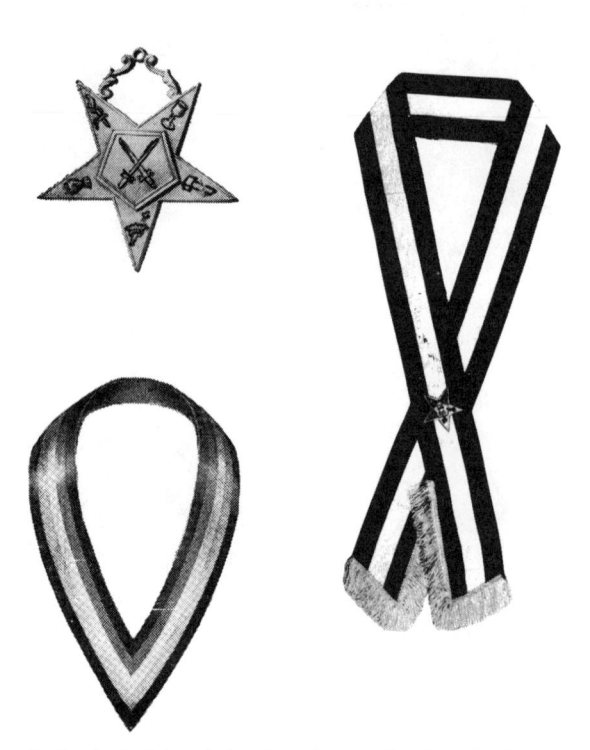

If the Sentinel is a lady, she will wear the five-colored sash, but should the Sentinel be a gentleman, the five-colored collar is proper.

JEWELS AND REGALIA

Adah

ADOPTIVE RITE RITUAL

Ruth

JEWELS AND REGALIA

Esther

ADOPTIVE RITE RITUAL

Martha

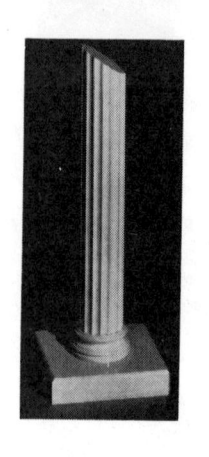

JEWELS AND REGALIA 47

Electa

CHAPTER PARAPHERNALIA

Every Chapter SHOULD HAVE the following:

1. Charter or Dispensation.
2. By-laws.
3. Seal with the name, number and location of the Chapter. Such seal shall be used for necessary official purposes: certificates, dimits, dues books or cards, summons, etc.
4. Signet with the emblematic Star for a complete explanation of the degrees and shall be placed in the East to the left of the Worthy Patron.
5. Register of Membership in which the Secretary shall record the name of each member, residence, date of initiation or affiliation, name, number and location of the Masonic Lodge with the Master Mason's name through whom the membership was gained. Date and cause of the termination of membership in the Chapter must also be recorded.
6. Minute or Record Book of the proceedings of the Chapter.
7. Secretary and Treasurer Cash Books and Receipts for Dues; Orders on Treasurer.
8. Dues Books or Dues Cards.
9. Altar in the center of the room with Altar Cloth.
10. One or more small Bibles.
11. Altar Bible with Marker.

CHAPTER PARAPHERNALIA

12. United States Flag.
13. Pedestal, or table for the Matron.
14. Gavels.
15. Ballot Box with white balls enough for the membership and at least a half-dozen black balls or black cubes.
16. Veils for Candidates.
17. Sword and Veil for Adah.
18. Wheat for Ruth.
19. Crown and Scepter for Esther.
20. Broken Column for Martha.
21. Cup for Electa.

OPTIONAL

22. Emblematic Star Floor Carpet.
23. Station Banners for the Five Star Points.
24. Banners bearing the words Truth, Faith, Wisdom and Charity.
25. Pedestals and Covers.
26. Christian Flag.
27. O.E.S. Flag.
28. Chapter Banner with name and number and emblematic Star.
29. Batons for Conductresses and Marshal.

CHAPTER MEETINGS

The meetings of the Chapter are *Regular* (Stated) or *Special*.

The *Regular* meetings are those held on a day and time fixed by the By-laws at which all regular business of the Chapter shall be transacted, and may be held weekly, semi-monthly, or monthly, at the choice of the members as expressed in the By-laws.

The *Special* meetings are those summoned at the will of the Worthy Matron or, in her absence, by the Associate Matron, when necessity requires. No business is proper at a *Special* meeting except such as is stated in the call.

The ballot upon petitions for the degrees of membership can be taken only at a *Regular* meeting, but the conferring of the degrees may take place at a *Special* meeting.

No meeting, either *Regular* or *Special*, is lawfully held unless the Charter, or Dispensation, is present.

The *place* of meeting may be held in a hall or private apartment. It must be sufficiently secluded to insure secrecy. An adjoining room, or anteroom, for the preparation of candidates and the reception of visitors, is essential.

QUORUM FOR BUSINESS

A meeting of the Chapter, for any business except conferring degrees, may be opened and held by *seven* members, the Worthy Matron or Associate Matron being one. The number proper to confer the degrees must be at least *nine,* of which the Worthy Patron or a Master Mason shall be one.

USE OF THE GAVEL

One blow of the gavel calls the Chapter to order, seats it when standing, establishes a decision, and completes the closing of the Chapter. *

Two blows call up the officers. * *

Three blows call up everyone in the room. * * *

RAPS

When giving an alarm at the door, five raps * * * * * shall be given, which shall be answered by five * * * * * from the other side. The door is opened by the Warder.

ADMISSION OF VISITORS

Only those who have received all the light of the Order can be present when the Chapter is opened and ready for business.

The officers of the Chapter are enjoined by every principle of prudence and self-preservation, to study critically the most thorough measures of precaution; to exercise extraordinary vigilance in purging the assemblies; and to allow neither fear nor favor to bias them in the admission of unworthy or unenlightened visitors. Not only will the honor of the Order suffer by any relaxation in these particulars, but wounds not easily healed may be inflicted upon the peace and happiness of the members.

Visitors and those not known to the Sentinel should be asked to show their membership card and, if necessary, undergo the customary examination before being allowed to enter the Chapter while it is in session.

Since a member of the Order visiting a Chapter, not her or his own, does so by courtesy, it is proper for the Worthy Matron to ask any or all Brothers and Sisters not members of that Chapter to retire from the room on those rare occasions when it would be embarrassing to discuss private Chapter matters before others than the Chapter's own members. No member of the Order, except an officer of the Grand Chapter, in the performance of an official duty, can of right claim admittance to any Chapter of which he or she is not a member. The right to visit is one of courtesy and may be denied at the pleasure of any member present. Such member who may object to the presence of a visiting member must make such objection in writing under his or her own signature to the presiding officer and such objection shall be given immediate attention and the visitor objected to shall be asked to retire from the Chapter before any further transaction of business.

OPENING CEREMONIES

(Without Flag Bearers)

The hour specified in the By-laws (or indicated in the summons when the meeting is a special one) for opening the Chapter having arrived, the furniture and paraphernalia of the Chapter being in place, the members assembled, the officers, with exception of the Worthy Patron, the Associate Patron (if authorized as an officer), the Associate Conductress, and the Musician, retire to the ante-room. The Associate Patron, the Associate Conductress and the Musician assume their stations. The Worthy Patron ascends the dais in the East[1] and gives one blow (*) with the gavel which is the signal for those in the room to come to attention and says:

W. P.—Sister Associate Conductress.

A. COND.—(*rises*) Worthy Patron.

W. P.—You will invite the Worthy Matron and other officers to enter the Chapter room.

A. C. goes to the door where the W. M. and officers are lined up and says:

---

[1] *That end of the room which is occupied by the presiding officer is termed the* East. *During the entrance of the officers, good effect may be produced by the use of music.*

A. COND.—By order of the Worthy Patron, I invite the Worthy Matron and the other officers to enter the Chapter room.

If the flag or flags are already placed in their positions in the East and there are no Flag Bearer officers (see page 71 for Opening with Flag Bearers), the officers enter in two lines, led by the C. and A. C. and take the positions as shown in the following diagram. Chaplain may enter from either side just before W. M. and A. M., carrying closed Bible. Places closed Bible on altar when officers are instructed to resume their stations.

A. C.		COND.
TREAS.		SEC'Y.
TRUSTEE		MARSHAL
ELECTA		TRUSTEE
MARTHA		ADAH
ESTHER	ALTAR	RUTH
CHR. OF T.	[CHAPLAIN]	WARDER
	W. M. A. M.	

As the officers enter, the Chapter is called up by the W. P. with *** (three blows of the gavel).

W. P.—Sisters Conductress and Associate Conductress, escort the Worthy Matron to the East.

Conductresses turn, march to W. M. and escort her to the East. W. P. hands the gavel to the Matron who says:

OPENING CEREMONIES 55

W. M.—The officers will resume their several stations and prepare for the active duties of the Chapter.

They do so. The Sentinel closes the door and sees that the ante-room is secured. When all is in readiness the Matron will say:

W. M.—Sisters and Brothers of .... Chapter No. .... and visitors of the Order of the Eastern Star, the hour has arrived for us to resume our labors. To open our Chapter in a manner that will insure the solemnity of our work, and to secure the best results, I must require your uninterrupted attention and assistance. Sister Associate Matron,[1] ascertain whether all present are members of the Order of the Eastern Star, or entitled to be present.

A. M.—Sister Conductress, ascertain and report if all present are members of the Order of the Eastern Star, or entitled to be present.

The Conductress and Associate Conductress will use the customary means of examination, by passing around the room, if necessary, to question those with whom they are not personally acquainted, beginning at the East, on the South and North. When fully satisfied, they resume their stations and the Cond. reports:

---

[1] *As each officer is addressed by the presiding officer, she rises without further signal, and remains standing during the ceremonies of opening.*

COND.—Sister Associate Matron, all Sisters present are members of the Order of the Eastern Star and entitled to be present.

A. M.—Worthy Matron, all Sisters present are members of the Order of the Eastern Star and entitled to be present.

If a visiting Sister is without the password and cannot answer the customary questions, the following report will be made to the A. M.: "Sister Associate Matron, I find a visitor in the North (or South) without the password (OR for whom I cannot vouch)." The A. M. will inquire if any person in the room can vouch for this Sister if she cannot do so herself. If no one present can vouch for the visitor, the A. M. will report to the W. M. by saying: "Worthy Matron, there is a Sister without the password (OR for whom I cannot vouch)." Whereupon the W. M. must request the visitor to retire with an examining committee (which she appoints immediately) under the escort of the Marshal. If the visitor cannot satisfactorily pass the examining committee's questions, she cannot be admitted.

The Patron will assure himself that the gentlemen present are entitled to seats in the Chapter, and so announce the fact to the W. M. If there should be any Master Masons present who have not been obligated, that ceremony should be performed immediately after the Chapter shall be declared open.

W. M.—It is well. In behalf of the Chapter, I extend a hearty welcome to all. Sister Warder,

OPENING CEREMONIES 57

you will instruct the Sentinel that we are engaged in the solemn ceremonies of opening our Chapter, and direct (her)[1] him to permit no interruption to be made while we are thus engaged.

The Warder opens the door and repeats the directions of the W. M. She then closes the door and says:

WAR.—Worthy Matron, no interruption will be made from without.

W. M.—Sister Associate Matron, what number of officers constitute a Chapter of the Order of the Eastern Star when complete, and what titles do they bear?

A. M.—A complete Chapter requires fifteen,[2] and their titles are: Worthy Matron, Worthy Patron, Associate Matron, (*Associate Patron*), Treasurer, Secretary, Conductress, Associate Conductress, (*3 Trustees*), Marshal, (*Musician*), (*Flag Bearers*), Warder, Sentinel, Adah, Ruth, Esther, Martha and Electa.

W. M.—Where is our Sentinel stationed?

A. M.—Outside the closed door.

W. M.—What are his duties? and explain his badge of office.

---

[1] *The Sentinel may, at the option of the Chapter, be a Sister or Brother; the latter is preferable.*
[2] *This number will depend on whether or not these officers are authorized: Associate Patron, 3 Trustees, Musician, Christian Flag Bearer, U.S. Flag Bearer, O.E.S. Flag Bearer, and Chaplain, and should be changed accordingly.*

A. M.—To protect the Chapter against the introduction of improper persons. His badge of office, the Cross-swords within the Star, emblems of protection, admonishes him that upon his watchful care depends our security against interruption, without which the solemnity of our proceedings would be destroyed and all secrecy lost.

W. M.—Where is our Warder stationed?

A. M.—At the Southwest entrance of the Chapter, Worthy Matron.

W. M.—What are your duties, Sister Warder? and explain your badge of office.

WAR.—To act in conjunction with the Sentinel in protecting the Chapter from the intrusion of improper persons. My badge of office, the Dove within the Star, an emblem of peace, admonishes me that a state of harmony and serenity becomes all our proceedings, and that I should use my utmost endeavors to promote it.

W. M.—Where is the Associate Conductress stationed?

WAR.—In the North, Worthy Matron.

W. M.—What are your duties, Sister Associate Conductress? and explain your badge of office.

A. C.—To receive and prepare candidates for initiation, and to assist the Conductress in the active duties of the Chapter. My badge of office, the Baton within the Star, an emblem of direction, admonishes me that good discipline is essential to the success of our society. My own attention to the directions of my superior officers will be the measure of respect which others will pay to me.

W. M.—Where is our Conductress stationed?

A. C.—In the South, Worthy Matron.

W. M.—What are your duties, Sister Conductress? and explain your badge of office.

COND.—To ascertain if all persons are entitled to be present at the opening of the Chapter, and to conduct candidates during their initiation. My badge of office, the Scroll and Baton, emblems of prepared plans and their fulfillment, admonishes me that the first impressions made upon a candidate, when entering our Chapter, are permanent, and should be for good; and that it depends greatly upon the manner of conducting her through the mazy labyrinth of our Rite, to make those impressions lasting and what we desire they should be.

W. M.—Where is our Secretary stationed?

COND.—In the Southeast, Worthy Matron.

W. M.—What are your duties, Sister Secretary? and explain your badge of office.

SEC.—To carefully observe the proceedings of the Chapter; to record that which is proper to be written; to receive all monies due the Chapter and pay the same to the Treasurer, taking her receipt therefor. My badge of office, the Crossed Pens within the Star, emblems of power and intelligence, admonishes me that as a faithful record is kept by an invisible pen of all our thoughts and actions, so I must be faithful to my trust, that the good deeds of my companions may not go unrecorded, and that the monies intrusted to my hands shall have proper record and direction.

W. M.—Where is our Treasurer stationed?

SEC.—In the Northeast, Worthy Matron.

W. M.—What are your duties, Sister Treasurer? and explain your badge of office.

TREAS.—To receive all monies from the Secretary, giving her a receipt therefor, and pay them out only upon an order signed by the Worthy Matron and Secretary. My badge of office, the Crossed Keys within the Star, emblems of security, admonishes me to the strictest fidelity in the preservation and disbursement of the funds intrusted to my keeping. The relief of the distressed, and the necessary expenses of our Chapter would be forfeited by a violation of the sacred obligations assumed by me.

(The following in italics is optional, depending on the authorization of such officers. If these officers are not used omit.)

W. M.—Where are our Trustees stationed?

TREAS.—The Chairman of the Trustees is stationed at the right of the Associate Matron; the other two are stationed near the Treasurer and Secretary, respectively.

W. M.—What are your duties, Sister Chairman? and explain your badge of office.

CHR. OF TRUSTEES—*The Trustees are the custodians of the property, regalia, investments and securities of the Chapter and are subject to the direction of the Chapter in all matters. Our badge of office, the Key within the Star, admonishes us to guard and protect the interests of the Chapter.*

W. M.—Where are our Flag Bearers stationed?

CHR. OF TRUSTEES—*To the right of the Worthy Matron in the East, at the foot of the dais.*

If O.E.S. Flag Bearer also, she will say: "To the right of the Worthy Matron and the left of the Worthy Patron in the East at the foot of the dais."

W. M.—What are your duties, Sisters Flag Bearers? and explain your badges of office.

CHRISTIAN F. B.—*My duty is to carry the Christian Flag which takes precedence over all others and to place it in the East. My badge of office, the Christian Flag within the Star, is the banner of the Prince of Peace. It stands for no one creed or denomination. The cross of red upon the blue field and white ground reminds me that upon the cross Christ made the supreme sacrifice that we might have the assurance of immortal life.*

U.S. F. B.—*My duty is to carry the Flag of the United States of America and to place it in its honored position in the East. My badge of office, the Flag within the Star, is a symbol of liberty and justice for all and reminds me that patriotism is essential in good citizenship.*

O.E.S. F. B.—My duty is to carry the Eastern Star Flag and to place it in the East. My badge of office, the Eastern Star Flag within the Star, is symbolic of the characters of the Five Heroines and reminds me that I should practice the lessons of those Heroines in my daily life.

W. M.—*Our Chaplain is stationed to the right of the Worthy Matron in the East, at the foot of the dais. Sister Chaplain, what are your duties and explain your badge of office.*

CHAP.—*My duty is to lead the Chapter in its devotion, to invoke the blessings of our Heavenly Father upon our work and to perform such other duties as are appropriate to my office. My badge is the Open Bible within the Star, an emblem of the Word of God, admonishing me to walk uprightly that my life may be void of offense toward God and man.*

W. M.—Where is our Marshal stationed?

F. B.—To the left of the Worthy Patron, at the foot of the dais.

W. M.—What are your duties, Sister Marshal? and explain your badge of office.

MAR.—My duty is (*to escort the flag[s]*), to respond to the roll call of officers, and to conduct the processions of the Chapter. My badge of office, the Crossed Batons within the Star, is a symbol of

OPENING CEREMONIES

order and discipline and reminds me that diligence is essential in the performance of duty.

W. M.—Where is our Musician stationed?

MAR.—At the organ (OR *piano*), *Worthy Matron.*

W. M.—What are your duties, Sister Musician? and explain your badge of office.

MUS.—My duty is to furnish the music for the ceremonies and enjoyment of the Chapter. My badge of office, the Lyre within the Star, is a symbol of music and poetry and reminds me that harmony is essential in the work of our Order.

W. M.—Where is Adah stationed?

MUS.—At the first point of the Star, Worthy Matron.

W. M.—Sister Adah, communicate to us the duties of your station, and explain the color and emblems appropriate to the blue point of our central Star.

ADAH—To make known to all proper inquirers the light, knowledge, and beauty of the blue ray, which represents the clearness of the sky, when all couds have vanished, and symbolizes chastity, loyalty, fidelity, and a spotless reputation. My emblems are the Sword and Veil, emblematic of the heroic conduct of Jephthah's Daughter, whom I represent.

W. M.—Where is Ruth stationed?

ADAH—At the second point of the Star, Worthy Matron.

W. M.—Sister Ruth, communicate to us the duties of your station, and explain the color and emblem appropriate to the yellow point of our central Star.

RUTH—To make known to all proper inquirers the light, knowledge, and beauty of the yellow ray, which symbolizes constancy, purity, and the lustre of great brightness. My badge, the Sheaf, is an emblem of plenty, which being composed of distinct and minute parts, is gathered together by patient industry. Such was the generous labor of the humble gleaner Ruth, whom I represent.

W. M.—Where is Esther stationed?

RUTH—At the third point of the Star, Worthy Matron.

W. M.—Sister Esther, communicate to us the duties of your station, and explain the color and emblems appropriate to the white point of our central Star.

ESTHER—To make known to all proper inquirers the light, knowledge, and beauty of the white ray, which symbolizes light, purity, and joy. My badge, the Crown and Scepter united, is an emblem of royalty and power. In the exercise of high authority, we should be governed by the purest principles of justice and moderation. It was by the practice of these attributes that Esther, whom I represent, saved her people from extirpation.

W. M.—Where is Martha stationed?

ESTHER—At the fourth point of the Star, Worthy Matron.

W. M.—Sister Martha, communicate to us the duties of your station, and explain the color and emblem appropriate to the green point of our central Star.

MARTHA—To make known to all proper inquirers the light, knowledge, and beauty of the green ray, the purity and freshness of which are emblems of delight—the beauties of nature—symbolizing hope and immortality. My badge, the Broken Column, is typical of the death of a human being, cut off in the vigor of manhood, and expresses the sisterly grief of Martha, whom I represent.

W. M.—Where is Electa stationed?

MARTHA—At the fifth point of the Star, Worthy Matron.

W. M.—Sister Electa, communicate to us the duties of your station, and explain the color and emblem appropriate to the red point of our central Star.

ELECTA—To make known to all proper inquirers the light, knowledge, and beauty of the red ray, symbolically representing ardor and zeal, which should actuate all who are engaged in the holy cause of benevolence. My badge, the Cup, is an emblem of the bitter draught of which we are constantly partaking through life but, however distasteful, will, in the end, overflow with blessings, rich, abounding, and eternal.

W. M.—Where is our Associate Patron stationed?
ELECTA—In the West, Worthy Matron.
W. M.—What are your duties, Brother Associate Patron? and explain your badge of office.
A. P.—My duty is to perform the duties of the Worthy Patron in his absence, and to give him whatever assistance may be required in the discharge of his duties. My badge of office, the Rayed Star within the Star, is an emblem of Divine Guidance.

W. M.—Where is our Associate Matron stationed?

A. P.—In the West, Worthy Matron.

W. M.—What are your duties, Sister Associate Matron? and explain your badge of office.

A. M.—To assist the Worthy Matron in the discharge of her duties, and to preside during her absence. My badge of office, the Refulgent Sun within the Star, an emblem of brightness, admonishes me to assist the Worthy Matron by my counsel, as the rising sun enlightens the day, being ever ready to assume her station, should she be absent.

OPENING CEREMONIES

W. M.—Where is our Worthy Patron stationed?

A. M.—In the East, at your left, Worthy Matron.

W. M.—What is his duty? and explain his badge of office.

A. M.—To preside during the conferring of the degrees and at other times when requested to do so by the Worthy Matron; to act as her advisor; to exercise a general supervision over the affairs of the Chapter and to see that the officers are proficient in their work. His badge of office, the Square and Compasses within the Star, is a symbol of his relationship to the Masonic Fraternity and the Order of the Eastern Star.

W. M.—Where is the Worthy Matron stationed?

A. M.—In the East, Worthy Matron.

W. M.—Explain her duties, responsibilities, and badge of office.

A. M.—To preside over the deliberations, and see that the purposes of the Chapter are properly conducted. Her badge of office, the Gavel within the Star, the highest emblem of authority, admonishes her that upon her judgment and discretion rests the government of this Chapter, and the prosperity of our beautiful Order in this place. Her responsibilities to God for the faithful discharge of her duties in this Chapter, and to her Sisters for the dissemination of light and knowledge, should ever prompt her to do her work in a spirit of faith and prayer.

W. M.—It is in this spirit that I propose to open our Chapter, and perform whatever duties may devolve upon me; and that we may have the needed grace to do our work well, let us pray. ° ° °

The W. Matron calls up the Chapter with three raps of the Gavel, when the Patron or Chaplain offers the following:

PRAYER

O Lord of all mercies and blessings! commend us, we beseech Thee at this time, in taking upon ourselves the work of extending the reign of peace and love upon earth. Grant us, first a willing mind which Thou wilt accept according to that which we have; and then, such ability from Thy hand that we may add honors to the noble cause we have here espoused. Bless our humble labors to the promotion of truth and love, unity and peace. Make all grace to abound toward us. Enrich us in everything to all bountifulness, that, through us, there may be thanksgiving unto Thee, our God. Amen.

W. M.—You have all spoken well and given utterance to noble sentiments. The pleasing thoughts, so beautifully expressed, are embodied in our Opening Hymn, in which I request you all to join.

While standing, all will join in singing the

OPENING CEREMONIES 69

OPENING ODE
AIR—"One day nearer Home"

Words by Bro. Robt Morris. Ar. by Bro. Henry Tucker.

1. Be-gin the work of praise, The joys of song be-gin; And bid the mys-tic-al rays To en-ter in.

Cho.—*Repeat pp*

The gleaming light, the guiding light, The light that shines a-far. It yields a radiance pure and bright. The beautiful, beau-ti-ful Star.

It tells of deathless Love,
  And Faith and Hope sublime;
It lifts the soul above
  All things of time.
    Cho.—The gleaming light, etc.

Then let the song of praise
  Our evening tasks begin;
And bid the mystical rays
  To enter in.
    Cho.—The gleaming light, etc.

At the conclusion of the singing the Matron says:

W. M.—In the name of the departed heroines whose virtues we should strive to emulate, in the name of our great Sisterhood, knit together in bonds of charity and sincere friendship, and in the name of our Heavenly Father, Who hath assured us that He loveth a cheerful giver, I declare *EAS* Chapter, No. *23* Order of the Eastern Star, open and in due order for the dispatch of business. Sister Warder, you will so instruct the Sentinel. Sister Associate Conductress, attend at the Altar.

The A. C. opens the Bible upon the Altar; the W. M. calls the Chapter to order (*). The Warder informs the Sentinel that the Chapter is open, and the business of the meeting proceeds. See page 75 for Order of Business.

OPENING CEREMONIES WITH FLAG BEARER(S)

If there are Flag Bearer officers, it is effective to have the flags carried into the room, escorted by the Marshal, before the officers start to march. (It would be improper for others to march while the flag is moving and all those already in the Chapter room should place their right hand on the left breast while the flag is in motion.)

Flag Bearers may march in, going inside the chairs, directly to the East in front of the W. P. where they would all turn simultaneously and face West which would be the cue for the other officers to start marching in. Note that if the Christian Flag is used, it must always have the position nearest the North and comes first as follows:

C. flag   U.S. flag   O.E.S. flag   Marshal

If only two flags are used the officers would line up as follows:

    C. flag   Marshal   U.S. flag, *or*
U.S. flag   Marshal   O.E.S. flag, *or*
         U.S. flag   Marshal

If preferred, the Flag Bearers and Marshal may march to a position west of the Altar and remain standing there while other officers enter and take positions as indicated in the diagram under "Opening Ceremonies." In either case, they remain in such positions until the W. M. announces that the flag (or flags) will be escorted to the East.

W. P.—Sister Associate Conductress.

A. COND.—(*rises*) Worthy Patron.

W. P.—You will invite the Worthy Matron and other officers to enter the Chapter room.

A. C. goes to the door where the W. M. and officers are lined up and says:

A. COND.—By order of the Worthy Patron, I invite the Worthy Matron and the other officers to enter the Chapter room.

W. P.—*** (*calling up all those in the room*).

Flag Bearers with escort of Marshal enter as outlined above and stand in position. Other officers then enter.

W. P.—Sisters Conductress and Associate Conductress, escort the Worthy Matron to the East.

They do so and Patron hands the Matron the gavel.

W. M.—The officers will resume their several stations and prepare for the active duties of the Chapter.

They do so and Sentinel closes the door. When all have reached their stations, the W. M. will say:

W. M.—Sisters and Brothers, we will pledge allegiance to the Flag of the United States of America.

ALL—I pledge allegiance to the Flag of the United States of America and to the Republic for

OPENING CEREMONIES WITH FLAG BEARER(S) 73

which it stands, one nation indivisible with liberty and justice for all.

During the pledge, the W. M. and W. P. step down from the dais and all face the flag and place right hand on left breast. Following the pledge, all join in singing one or more verses of the "Star Spangled Banner."

W. M. and W. P. then resume their stations and the flags are placed in stands provided for them on the dais. The Christian Flag is the only one in the world which takes precedence over the U.S. Flag and is placed nearest to the Treasurer. These are the proper positions:

Tr.   CF.   USF.   WM   WP   Signet   OESF.   Sec'y

At the end of the singing, Flag Bearer(s) and Marshal march to their stations, Marshal and O.E.S. Flag Bearer marching along North side to West, turn and march South, turn and march East, to their seats in front of the W. P. The Christian and U.S. Flag Bearers do not march as they are already by their stations.

If Flag Bearers have marched in to West of the Altar, they remain in that position until the W. M. has taken her station and directed the officers to resume theirs. She will then say:

W. M.—Sisters and Brothers, the flag(s) will be escorted to its (their) position(s) of honor in the East.

All present place right hand over left breast as soon as the flag is in motion and when Flag Bearer(s) has reached the East at the foot of the dais, they with Marshal turn simultaneously and face West. W. M. and W. P. step down and W. M. will say:

"*Sisters and Brothers, we will pledge allegiance,*" *etc.*

From this point include all material in "Opening Ceremonies" pages 55–71, beginning:

W. M.—Sisters and Brothers of _____ Chapter No. __ and visitors of the Order of the Eastern Star, the hour has arrived, etc.

ORDER OF BUSINESS

1. Opening Ceremonies.
2. Calling Roll of Officers.
3. Reading the Minutes of the last meeting.
4. Sickness and Distress.
5. Reports on Candidates proposed.
6. Balloting for Candidates.
7. Petitions for Membership.
8. Conferring Degrees.
9. Reading Communications.
10. Unfinished Business.
11. New Business.
12. Reports of Special Committees.
13. Reports of Standing Committees.
14. Reading and Approving Bills.
15. Reading and Approving of Minutes.
16. Closing Ceremonies.

Note: Election and Installation of Officers should take place immediately after No. 4—Sickness and Distress.

This Order of Business may be changed by the Worthy Matron, no member objecting.

CLOSING CEREMONIES

The business of the Chapter being completed, the Worthy Matron proceeds as follows:

W. M.—Sister Associate Matron, does any work of charity or benevolence remain unperformed?

A. M.—None, Worthy Matron, within my knowledge.

W. M.—Then, Sister Warder, you will instruct the Sentinel that we are about to close this Chapter, and to permit no interruption to be made while we are thus engaged.

*Warder gives *****. Sentinel responds with *****. Warder opens the door and informs the Sentinel:*

WAR.—Brother (*or Sister*) Sentinel, the Worthy Matron directs me to inform you that we are about to close this Chapter and to permit no interruption to be made while we are thus engaged.

SENTINEL—Sister Warder, inform the Worthy Matron that there will be no interruption.

CLOSING CEREMONIES

Warder closes the door and reports:

WAR.—Worthy Matron, no interruption will be made from without.

W. M.—It is well. Sisters and Brothers, unite with us in singing our Closing Ode.

The W. M. calls up the Chapter ***.

CLOSING ODE

AIR—"Home, sweet Home."

Words by Bro. ROBT. MORRIS.   Ar. by Bro. HENRY TUCKER.

Chorus or Duett.

The Star we have followed now sinks in the west, but leaves in our hearts all its mem-o-ries blest, As spring yields to sum-mer, yet fades not its

[Sheet music: "bloom: So bear we these mem-o-ries... joy-ful-ly home. Home, home, sweet, sweet home, We praise Thee, our Fa-ther, who giv-eth a home."]

When called from earth's labor to lands far away,
Where sorrow is pleasure and darkness is day,
  May all now departing in harmony come,
  And bloom in God's presence with angels at home.
    Home, home, sweet, sweet home!
We praise Thee, our Father, who giveth a home!

At the conclusion of the singing, the Matron says:

W. M.—Sisters and Brothers, we will unite in prayer.

CLOSING CEREMONIES

PATRON (or CHAP.)—Holy and Most Merciful Father, Who answers prayers, bestow upon us a parting blessing, and grant that we may remember the vows we have assumed; cause us to remember our obligations to each other and to Thee. Help us to practice out of the Chapter the lessons we have here learned that we may live in peace and harmony with our fellow-men. May Thy protecting care be about us until we meet again. Amen.

ALL—Amen.

W. M.—Sister Conductress, attend at the altar.

Conductress closes the Holy Bible upon the altar and returns to her station.

W. M.—Sisters and Brothers, we go forth into the world, not knowing the things that shall meet us there, save that troubles and trials everywhere abound in the labyrinth of human life. Let us never be dismayed, for our Heavenly Father has promised to strengthen us, to help us, and to uphold us with the right hand of His power. I now declare .... Chapter No. .... closed. Sister Warder, you will so inform the Sentinel.

Warder opens the door and informs the Sentinel:

WAR.—Brother (*or Sister*) Sentinel, the Worthy Matron directs me to inform you that the Chapter is closed.

Warder closes the door and says:

WAR.—Worthy Matron, the Sentinel has been informed that the Chapter is closed.

W. M.—Farewell.

ALL—Farewell.

W. M.—* (*one blow of the gavel*).

CLOSING CEREMONIES WITH RETIRING OF FLAG(S)

Follow "Closing Ceremonies" pages 76–79, to and including:

W. M.—Sister Conductress, attend at the Altar.

Cond. closes the Holy Bible upon the Altar and returns to her station.

W. M.—Sisters and Brothers, attention. The Flag(s) will be retired under the escort of the Marshal.

Flag Bearer(s) remove flag or flags from their stands, holding them at right side in vertical position, close to the body in front of right shoulder. Face the West, while all sing "America." At the end of one or two verses, Flag Bearer(s) and Marshal march abreast to Altar; wheel right, facing North, turn West and march out preparation room door (the Sentinel should have the door open and be ready to take the flags). Flag Bearer(s) and Marshal then return to their stations, Christian and U.S. Flag

CLOSING CEREMONIES 81

Bearers return along the North side of the room and the Marshal and O.E.S. Flag Bearer along the South side. Flag Bearers on the North will wait until Marshal and O.E.S. Flag Bearer have reached the Southwest corner of room so that they can all march East at the same time.

From this point include all material in "Closing Ceremonies" pages 79–80 to the end.

DIAGRAM FOR RETIRING OF FLAGS
East

(1)	(2)	(3)	(4)
C. F. B.	U.S. F. B.	O.E.S. F. B.	Mar.

```
                                1 2 3 4
                                1 2 3 4
              1 2 3 4  ←  1 2 3 4
                 ↓            (Altar)
                 4
                 3
                 2
                 1
              (Door)
```

BALLOTING

According to No. 8 and No. 9 of THE LAND-MARKS, each candidate for membership shall be unanimously elected by ballot at a *Stated* or *Regular* meeting and the character of the ballot cast by a member shall be kept inviolably secret. It is the right of every Chapter to be the judge of who shall be admitted to its membership.

All members who are present in their Chapter room at the time of balloting are entitled to one vote each on Candidates for the degrees or for affiliation.

When Balloting is reached in the Order of Business, the W. M. will say:

W. M.—Sister Associate Conductress, prepare the ballot box.

The A. C. should have the box by her chair. She will examine it to see that there are a sufficient number of white balls and at least six black cubes or balls.

A. COND.—Worthy Matron, the ballot box is prepared.

W. M.—Sister Associate Conductress, convey the ballot box to the East for inspection.

A. C. carries the box to the East, marching by way of the West then to the East. W. M. and W. P. examine the box. W. P. will hold it while A. C. stands at the foot of dais and W. M. says:

BALLOTING

W. M.—Sisters and Brothers of ...... Chapter No. ..., we are about to ballot upon the petition of ...... for membership in this Chapter. Each member in favor of granting the prayer of the petitioner will cast a white ball, and each opposed, a black cube (*or ball*).

W. M. and W. P. then cast their ballots and the box is handed to A. C.

W. M.—Sister Associate Conductress, convey the ballot box to the Associate Matron (*and Associate Patron*) in the West for her (*their*) ballot(s) and then place the ballot box upon the Altar.[1] Proceed to ballot and take your position behind the chair of Ruth. Sister Marshal, proceed to ballot and then guard the door to the preparation room.

A. C. and Marshal comply with W. M.'s instructions and will stand at these positions until W. M. declares the ballot closed.

W. M.—The officers will proceed to ballot.

Each member entitled to a vote shall approach the Altar from the West, between the chairs of Ruth and Esther, ballot, and leave between the chairs of Esther and Martha, and return to their seats. Each member must pause at the edge of the labyrinth while the preceding member is casting a ballot.

---

[1] *If the ballot box is passed around the room rather than placed on the Altar, the A.C. will carry the box to each member for her or his vote, and the above directions will be omitted to* "W.M.—Sister A.C., have all members balloted?"

W. M.—The members on the North will proceed to ballot.

When they have finished:

W. M.—The members on the South will proceed to ballot.

When all have balloted:

W. M.—Sister Associate Conductress, have all members balloted?
A. COND.—All the members have balloted, Worthy Matron.
W. M.—I declare the ballot closed. ° (*one blow of gavel*) Sister Associate Conductress, convey the ballot box West, then East, for the inspection.

A. C. carries the box to the A. M. (and A. P.) who inspect(s) it, then carries it to the East and hands it to the W. P. who inspects it as does the W. M.

W. M.—Sister Associate Matron, how is the ballot in the West?
A. M.—The ballot is clear in the West, Worthy Matron.
W. M.—Worthy Patron, how is the ballot in the East?
W. P.—The ballot is clear in the East, Worthy Matron.

W. M.—The ballot being clear, I have the pleasure to inform you that .... has been elected to become a member of this Chapter. * (one blow)

The Patron destroys the ballot by emptying all balls back into the box and hands it to A. C. who takes it and resumes her station. Marshal returns to her station.

If rejecting ballots appear in the ballot box, the A. M., after being asked how the ballot is in the West, will say:

A. M.—The ballot is cloudy in the West, Worthy Matron.

W. M.—How is the ballot in the East, Worthy Patron.

W. P.—The ballot is cloudy in the East, Worthy Matron.

W. M.—The ballot being cloudy, it is my duty to announce the petition of ...... rejected. * (one blow of gavel)

Note: If, on inspecting the ballot box, the W. M. and W. P. find only one black cube, the Matron, without asking the A. M. the result, will order a second and FINAL *ballot. Should a black cube or ball be found on the second ballot it may be safe to assume that no error was made by a member.*

INITIATION

The Secretary of the Chapter should notify all candidates who have been elected to receive the degrees well in advance of the meeting date, instructing them as to the time and place. The Sentinel will ask the candidates to remain in the ante-room until the proper time.

NOTE: *The initiation fee must be paid before conferring the degrees.*

When the Initiation Ceremony is reached in the Order of Business, the Matron will say:

W. M.—Sister Associate Conductress, you will retire and ascertain if there are any candidates in waiting, and report to the Worthy Patron.

The W. M. will now present the Gavel to the Patron, who takes charge of the Chapter.

The A. C. retires, and finding a candidate in the ante-room, ascertains her name, returns to the Chapter room, and says:

A. COND.—Worthy Patron, I find (*naming the person or persons*)[1] present and desirous of being initiated into our Order.

W. P.—Sister Secretary, has the petition of this candidate been received in open Chapter, and has she been regularly elected to receive the degrees of the Order?

SEC.—She has.

---

[1] *If there is more than one candidate, all the questions, etc., must be varied to suit the case.*

INITIATION

W. P.—Then, Sister Associate Conductress, you will again retire, and propound to the candidate the necessary questions, and, if satisfactorily answered, prepare her for the ceremonies of initiation, and, when so prepared, make the usual alarm at the door of the preparation-room.

The A. C. retires, and says to the candidate:

A. COND.—Do you still entertain the desire expressed in your petition, to receive the light and privileges of the Order of the Eastern Star?

CANDIDATE—I do.

A. COND.—It is well. Your request shall be complied with.

The A. C., taking the candidate into the preparation room, will say:

A. COND.—My friend, human life is a labyrinth through which we all wander blindly, and too often, alas, in ignorance. It is good to have a friend by our side and a friendly hand that can guide us with infallible certainty and safety through its intricate mazes. Permit me, therefore, for a time, to act as your guide, and to prepare you for the ceremonies of our Order.

The A. C. then prepares the candidate, by removing her hat, gloves, cloak or shawl, and jewelry, so that she will appear plainly dressed. A thin white veil is thrown over her head and face, and she is *led to the inner door of the Chapter, where the A. C. gives ***** distinct raps. The Conductress, rising in her station, says:*

COND.—Worthy Patron, there is an alarm at the door of the preparation room.

W. P.—Sister Conductress, ascertain the cause of the alarm, and ask the necessary questions.

The Conductress goes to the door, gives five distinct knocks *****, opens the door, and says:

COND.—Who knocks at the door of our Chapter?

A. COND.—The Associate Conductress, with a candidate who desires to be initiated into our Order.

COND.—Has the candidate made satisfactory answers to the necessary questions?

A. COND.—She has.

COND.—Is she properly prepared?

A. COND.—She is.

COND.—(*to the candidate*) My friend, have you well considered the request you make?

CANDIDATE—I have.

COND.—Are you prepared to undergo the necessary trials and assume our obligation of secrecy?

CANDIDATE—I am.

COND.—Are you also prepared faithfully to perform the duties and to accept the responsibilities of a Sister of the Eastern Star?

INITIATION

CANDIDATE—I am.

COND.—Learn then the first lesson of a petitioner. Be patient, and wait.

The Conductress closes the door, turns to the Patron, and says:

COND.—Worthy Patron, the alarm was caused by the Associate Conductress with the candidate, who desires to be initiated into our Order.

W. P.—Has she made satisfactory answers to the necessary questions?

COND.—She has.

W. P.—Then you will admit her.

Lights are dimmed except over the altar. Marshal proceeds to preparation room door so she can lead the march through the labyrinth and carries an open ritual in her hands so that she may prompt the officers if necessary.

The Conductress, opening the door, says:

COND.—Orders have been transmitted to me by our Worthy Patron, that this candidate be admitted into our Chapter, we having entire confidence in her integrity and fidelity. Enter, dear friend, for we are prepared to give you a hearty welcome.

As the candidate enters the door, the Conductress takes her by the left arm and with the Marshal leading, conducts her around the room, outside of the star, slow soft music being played. While making the cir-

cuit of the star, the Conductress will recite the following, or an Ode may be sung.

The A. C. resumes her station unless there is more than one candidate in which event she would escort the candidate last in line.

COND.—You have, doubtless, well considered the step you have taken in entering this Order.—It is dedicated to Charity, Truth, and Loving Kindness.—You come here of your own free choice. Complain not, therefore, at any trial.—A seal is set upon your lips.—Let it warn you to be ever silent and secret as to all that may befall you or be made known to you here.—Be not weary in well doing.—Woe unto those who seek to take upon themseves burdens which they are unable to bear. —Woe unto the faithless and insincere, who assume their obligations lightly, and forthwith forget them.—Trust in the Lord with all your heart, and lean not unto your own understanding.—In all your ways acknowledge Him, and He will direct your paths.

Having made the circuit, and reached the West, the Conductress will say:

COND.—Sister Associate Matron, I have the pleasure of introducing (*naming the person*), to be presented by you to the Worthy Patron. She declares herself prepared to assume our obligation of

INITIATION

secrecy, and faithfully to perform the duties of the Order of the Eastern Star.

A. M.—My friend, you are heartily welcome. Sister Conductress, cause the candidate to face the East.

The candidate is placed in position, facing the East, when the Associate Matron will say:

ASSOC. MATRON—Worthy Patron, I have the honor to introduce to you .... wife (*or sister, etc.*) of a Master Mason, whose petition has been approved by this Chapter; who now declares herself ready to enter upon the good work in which we are engaged, and to pledge her honor in our Covenant of Adoption for the faithful discharge of all its duties.

The Worthy Patron rises and addresses the Candidate.

W. P.—It is with great pleasure that I welcome you into this Chapter. The recommendations you bring have convinced us that you are a proper subject for the light of the Order of the Eastern Star. We trust that the lessons taught here will both please and instruct you. The objects for which we are associated together are to comfort, protect and aid each other in our journey through the labyrinth of human life, and to make its various hardships lighter by means of cheerful companionship and social pleasures. We are willing that you should join us in this pleasing work.

We are in possession of certain secrets, by means of which we recognize each other wherever we may meet. We are willing to make you acquainted with these secrets, that you, too, may be recognized as a member of this society. We are governed by a Supreme Grand Chapter, which makes our laws and regulations uniform with those of all other Subordinate Chapters of this Order, and by a form of by-laws framed by ourselves. We are bound to obey these laws, regulations and by-laws while we remain members of the society. In this obedience we shall expect you to share.

It becomes, then, my pleasing duty, as the representative of the highest responsible officer of this Chapter, to explain to you the nature of the Covenant of Adoption. It is the solemn pledge which you must give to this assembly before you can participate in the labors or enjoy the privileges of the Order. But we do not wish, nor would we permit you to assume this pledge save with your own consent, and with a full understanding of what is implied by it. If, after the Covenant is rehearsed, you should be unwilling to bind yourself thus solemnly, you may, without impediment or offense, retire from this place. It is as follows, and to all its parts we require your decided and unequivocal assent.

Sister Conductress, conduct the Candidate west of the Altar.

brought me very low. I have opened my mouth unto the Lord, and I cannot go back." Adah, casting aside the instruments of rejoicing, and with due solemnity, answered, "My father, if thou hast opened thy mouth unto the Lord, do to me according to that which hath proceeded out of thy mouth."

She had but one request to make and then she was ready for the sacrifice. She asked that she might go among the mountains for two months, and there, with her young friends, prepare her mind to meet, in calmness and resignation, her impending doom. The request was granted, and during two revolving moons, the heroic woman joined in the lamentations and devotions of her friends.

When the two months had expired, and the day arrived which was to bring this sad affair to a close, a vast multitude gathered together to witness the event. Precisely as the sun came on the meridian she was seen, followed by a long train of her friends, winding their way down the mountain's side, to the fatal spot where the altar was erected and her father, with an almost broken heart, was standing, prepared to fulfill his vow.

She approached him and, with one long kiss of affection, bade him farewell. Taking hold of the thick mourning veil which she wore, he drew it gently over her face and drew his sword. But she rapidly unveiled herself, and said she needed not to have her face covered, for *she was not afraid to die*. Her father replied that he could not strike the blow while she looked upon him, and again cast it over her. She threw it off the second time and, turning from him, said she would look up to the heavens, so that his hand should not be unnerved by the sight of her face, but that *she would not consent to die in the dark*. A third time, however, he insisted, and a third time she as resolutely cast it off, this time HOLDING THE ENDS OF IT FIRMLY IN HER HANDS, and then in the hearing of the multitude she solemnly declared that if this ceremony was insisted upon she would claim the protection of the law and refuse the fate that otherwise she was willing to endure. She said it was the practice to cover the faces of murderers and criminals when they were about to be put to death, but *she was no criminal, and died only to redeem her father's honor*. Again she averred that she would cast her eyes upward upon the Source of Light, and in that position she invited the fatal blow. It fell. Her gentle spirit mounted to the heavens upon which her last gaze had been fixed, and so the deed was consummated which has rendered the name of JEPHTHAH'S DAUGHTER forever famous in the annals of Scripture.

The sign of the degree is ___(1)___.[1]

---

[1] See syllabus for (1), etc.

INITIATION

The pass is __(2) Alas My daughter__

The color appropriate to the degree is BLUE, which we symbolize by the azure and hazy atmosphere that enveloped the mountains of Judea, in whose caves and solitude Jephthah's daughter dwelt with her companions two months while preparing for death. It also symbolizes fidelity, and should teach us to be faithful to all our obligations.

The emblems are the SWORD AND VEIL. By the sword, in the hands of the father, was the daughter slain. The veil alludes to the firmness with which Adah adhered to her determination to die in the light, suffering no stain to rest upon her memory after death.

You will now conduct our Sister to the second point of the Star for further instruction.

The Conductress proceeds with the Candidate to the second point of the Star, by passing around the point of Martha, to RUTH, *during which the following Ode may be sung:*

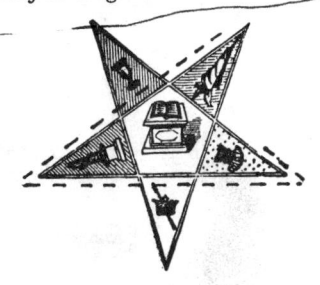

ADOPTIVE RITE RITUAL

TRIBUTE TO JEPHTHAH'S DAUGHTER

Music by Bro. HENRY TUCKER.

TRIBUTE TO JEPHTHAH'S DAUGHTER

See 'midst the multitude the VICTIM stands
  Dauntless, serene, though terror palsies them.
And she must die by her own father's hand!
  And she must die a sacrifice of shame!
Of shame? ah, no! she flings the veil abroad,
Once, twice, yea thrice; looks hopefully to God;
Fixes the noonday sun with earnest eyes,
Then crowned with innocence, the Maiden dies.

Lament for JEPHTHAH, ye who know his fate,
  Weep and lament; "Broken the beautiful rod,
And the strong staff; Mizpeh is desolate."
  But for sweet ADAH weep not; let the word
Be: "Joy to the Captive, freed from earthly dust,
Joy for one witness more to woman's trust.
And lasting honor, Mizpeh, be the strain
To HER WHO DIED IN LIGHT without a stain."

COND.—Sister Ruth, at the request of the Worthy Patron, I introduce to you our worthy Sister, to be instructed in the devotional respect due to religious principles, as illustrated in the history of Ruth.

RUTH—His request shall be complied with.

Ruth was of the nation of Moab, an idolatrous people. She married a man named Mahlon, formerly a native of Bethlehem, who had taken up his residence in the land of Moab, where he died. He was a worshiper of God, and by his pious example and teachings she was converted to the true religion. A few happy years followed, and then the calamity of widowhood came upon her. Upon his death-bed he solemnly exhorted her, for her soul's

sake, to leave the dangerous company in which she would be thrown, and go to the city of Bethlehem, where dwelt the people of God.

Immediately after his death, leaving her home and friends, she journeyed in company with her aged mother-in-law, Naomi, to Bethlehem, where she arrived in due time, way-worn and so poor that she was compelled, for her own support and that of her friend, to seek some means of securing a livelihood. There was nothing, however, that she could do save to go into the barley fields—for it was the time of harvest—and glean among the poorest and lowest classes of the people for a support. The very first attempt she made at this labor exhausted her strength. She had been reared in luxury, and the toil was too great for her. The sharp stubble wounded her feet. The blazing sun oppressed her brain. The jeers and insults of her companions alarmed and discouraged her, and just before the hour of noon, with only two little handsful of barley, as the fruits of her labor, she sought the shade of a tree to rest herself for a few moments before retiring from the field.

At this moment Boaz, the owner of the field, entered. He was a pious and charitable man. None in Bethlehem was so rich, none more beloved and honored than he. As he entered the field, he observed near the gleaners the form of one differing in garb and manners from the rest, and asked the overseer who she was. In reply he learned that she was a woman from Moab who had asked leave to glean among the sheaves, but that evidently she was unaccustomed to such labor, for she had been there since the sunrise and had gathered but two little handsful of barley. This excited the kindly feelings of Boaz, and he went to her to say a word of sympathy and to offer her relief.

As she saw him approach, she supposed him to be the owner of the field, coming to order her away. Ever since the morning she had met nothing but scorn and reproach, and she looked for it now. Raising her hands, therefore, to show him how small were her gleanings, and that she had taken nothing from the sheaves, she placed them meekly upon her breast, as showing her willingness to submit to whatever lot she might be called upon to endure, and cast her eyes upward as appealing to God against the inhumanity of man. It was for God she had forsaken home, wealth and friends and the disconsolate widow, alone in the world, had none other to whom she could look for protection. This mute appeal was not lost upon the kind heart of Boaz. He spoke words of sympathy and tenderness to her. He encouraged her to persevere. From the provisions brought for his reapers he bade her eat and drink. He directed that handsful of barley should be dropped on purpose in her way by the reapers, so that she might gather an ample supply. And when she returned home to her mother-in-law, she bore with her enough for their immediate necessities.

The sign of the degree is __(3)__.

The pass is __(4)__.

The color appropriate to the degree is YELLOW, which symbolizes the ripened grain in the field of Boaz, in which Ruth was an humble gleaner.

INITIATION

The S<small>HEAF</small> is an emblem of plenty, which, from its distinct and minute parts, teaches us that by patient industry, gleaning here a little and there a little, we may accumulate a competency to support us when the infirmities of age unfit us for the fatigues of labor.

You will now conduct our Sister to the third point of the Star for further instruction.

The Conductress proceeds with the Candidate around the point of Electa to the third point of the Star, to E<small>STHER</small>, *during which the following Ode may be sung:*

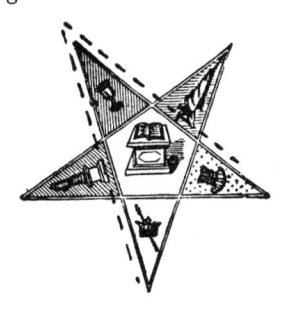

TRIBUTE TO RUTH

Music by Bro. Henry Tucker.

1. Widow, mourning for the dead, 'Midst the gold-en harvest mourning, Beats the sun thy ach-ing head? Burns the stub-ble 'neath thy tread? No kind look thy gaze re-turn-ing, These poor par-cels all thy store? Sure-ly God will give thee more, Sure-ly God will give thee more.

2. Stand, then, mournfully and sigh; Raise thy hands in meek sub-mis-sion; Thy Re-deem-er, Ruth, is nigh— Marks thee with a gra-cious eye, Knows thy lone-ly, sad con-di-tion; All thou'st giv-en him and more Shall be ren-dered from his store, Shall be ren-dered from his store.

COND.—Sister Esther, at the request of the Worthy Patron, I introduce to you our worthy Sister, to be instructed in that truly beautiful virtue, fidelity to kindred and friends, as exemplified in the history of Esther.

ESTHER—His request shall be complied with.

Esther was a Jewish damsel. Her family had not returned to Judea after the permission given by Cyrus, and she was born beyond the Tigris, about five hundred years before the Christian era. Her parents being dead, Mordecai, her cousin, took charge of her education. After Ahasuerus had divorced Queen Vashti, search was made throughout Persia for the most beautiful woman, and Esther was the one selected. She found favor in the eyes of the King, who married her with royal magnificence, bestowing largesses and remissions of tribute on his people.

Her matchless beauty having attracted the attention of the King, her virtues secured his love, but her wonderful genius gained his permanent admiration and respect. No woman has ever left behind her such a record of wisdom as Esther. It is a standing tradition among her people, that *as Solomon was to men so was Esther to women*, the wisest of her sex. The more intimately the King became acquainted with her mental powers, the more he respected them. There was no problem of state so intricate that she was not able to solve. In time she became his confidant, and shared with him in the greatness of his kingdom. These circumstances enabled her in a season of peril to save her nation from destruction.

The enemies of the Jews, who were numerous and powerful, had brought false accusations before the King, and persuaded him to promulgate an edict that, upon a fixed day, the entire race throughout all Persia should be exterminated. The chosen people of God were doomed to be extirpated from the face of the country. The instrument to avert so great a calamity was the heroine, Esther.

No sooner did she learn of this cruel edict than

she promptly resolved to save her people or perish in the same destruction. The King had often admitted his indebtedness to her counsels, and pledged his royal word to grant her any request she might make of him, even "to the half of the kingdom," and Esther now resolved to test his sincerity, and appeal to him, even at the risk of her own life, to reverse the horrible edict. She attired herself in her white silken robes, placed a brilliant crown upon her head, gathered her maidens around her, and went boldly, and in state, to the palace of the King.

It was a day of Grand Council, a gathering of the governors, princes, and officers of Persia. The dependent nations had sent in their deputations to pay homage and tribute, and the royal guards thronged the ante-chambers of the palace. It was a standing law of that place that none should enter the King's presence without summons, under penalty of death, and the sentinels, as the Queen passed, reminded her of this and warned her of her danger. But she bade them stand aside, and so, pale but firm, she passed through the vestibule into the great Council Chamber.

The scene was magnificent. The King upon his throne of gold and ivory; the gorgeous equipages of his officers, and the splendor of the apartment itself, all made up a display rarely equaled and never surpassed. Through all the crowd of courtiers, Esther boldly passed and, amidst the deathly silence of the observers, stood up before the King. Pale with fasting and sleeplessness, but not with fear, her cheeks emulated the whiteness of her silken robes. She fastened her eye fearlessly upon the King, who, angry at the violation of the law, frowned sternly upon her. It was the crisis of her life. The wise woman felt it to be so, and at once reminded him of his former pledges by a method *understood between them.* She saw his golden scepter bent toward her, and hastened to secure her pardon by coming forward, kneeling, and laying her hand upon it. Graciously said the King, "What wilt thou, Queen Esther? and what is thy request? It shall be given thee even to the half of the kingdom." The admiring crowds applauded the generosity of their monarch and, as he placed her beside him on the throne, gave utterance to their feelings in loud expressions of admiration at her beauty, discretion, and favor with the King.

The sacred narrative informs us of the consummate tact with which Esther pursued the advantage she had gained. She achieved a complete success and saved the nation, which, to this day, keeps an annual festival, Purim, in her honor.

The sign of the degree is __(5)__.

The pass is __(6)__.

The color appropriate to the degree is WHITE,

INITIATION

and alludes to the white silken robes in which Esther was dressed when she appeared before the King in the court of Persia. It is emblematical of the spotless purity of her character, and teaches us to be ever mindful of our rectitude of conduct in the affairs of life so as to be above the tongue of reproach.

The CROWN AND SCEPTER united is an emblem of royalty and power. It reminds us of the dignity of the King and the meek submission of the queenly petitioner.

You will now conduct our Sister to the fourth point of the Star for further instruction.

The Candidate is conducted around the point of Adah to the fourth point of the Star, to MARTHA, *during which the following Ode may be sung:*

TRIBUTE TO ESTHER

1. See, oh King, the suppliant one, Pale and trembling at the throne! See the gold-en crown she bears, And the silk-en robe she wears; Whiter, brighter than their sheen, Is the woman's soul with-in!

2. Mer-cy's gold-en wand ex-tend, While her gen-tle head shall bend: Meekly o'er thy scep-ter now, Par-don, fa-vor, boun-ty show, Naught in all thy broad domain, Like the woman's soul with-in!

INITIATION 113

COND.—Sister Martha, at the request of the Worthy Patron, I introduce to you our worthy Sister, to be instructed in the sublime virtue whereby we may display proper respect to undeviating faith in the hour of trial, as exemplified in the history of Martha.

MARTHA—His request shall be complied with.

The history of Martha is that of a young woman, oppressed with grief at the loss of an only brother. The family, composed of two sisters, Martha and Mary, with their brother Lazarus, were residents of Bethany. They were particularly known among the people of the country as *followers of Christ*.

Upon a certain occasion, during the absence of their Divine Master, Lazarus was taken suddenly and violently ill and, in a short time, died. At the close of the fourth day, intelligence reached them that Jesus was returning to Bethany. Martha hastened to meet Him, fell on her knees before Him, raised her hands imploringly toward his face, and, with a voice almost suppressed with emotion, cried aloud: "Lord, if Thou hadst been here, my brother had not died. But I know, that even now, whatsoever Thou wilt ask of God, God will give it Thee!"

Then said Jesus: "Thy brother shall rise again." She replied: "I know that he shall rise again in the resurrection at the last day."

Jesus said unto her: "I am the resurrection, and the life; he that believeth in me, though he were dead, yet shall he live; and whosoever liveth and believeth in me shall never die. Believest thou this?"

The sign of the degree is __(7)__.

The pass is __(8)__.

The color appropriate to the degree is GREEN, emblematical of the immutable nature of Truth and its victory. The Evergreen is the symbol of our faith in the immortality of the soul, and the realization of an everlasting happiness beyond the grave.

The BROKEN COLUMN is an expressive emblem of the uncertainty of human existence, and the outward evidence of the decease of a young man cut down in the vigor of life.

You will now conduct our sister to the fifth point of the Star for further instruction.

The Candidate is conducted around the point of Ruth to the fifth point of the Star, to ELECTA, *during which the following Ode may be sung:*

TRIBUTE TO MARTHA

Music by Bro. HENRY TUCKER.

1. Raise thy hands a-bove, sweet mourner, High - er,
2. He has wept for hu - man sor - row, Let thy

high-er, toward the throne! Ah, he sees thee,
sor-rows with him plead; Raise thy hands in

hears thy sto-ry, Hears and feels that plaintive moan.
faith, and doubt not, He hath pow-er 'o'er the dead.

COND.—Sister Electa, at the request of the Worthy Patron, I introduce to you our worthy Sister, to be instructed in the ever commendable virtue of patience and submission under wrongs, as exemplified in the history of Electa.

ELECTA—His request shall be complied with.

Electa was a lady of high repute in the land of Judea, of noble family, wealthy and accomplished, who lived in the days of St. John, the Evangelist, and was remarkable for her profuse benevolence to the poor. Electa had been educated in accord-

ance with the times and customs of the people who ruled the affairs of the country in which she lived. The idols of Rome were the only gods she had been taught to worship. Like Ruth, however, she had been rescued from the direful influences of heathenism, and from the abominations of that sinful system. Soon after the conversion of many of the people to the doctrines of Christ, she became converted to the belief of His power to save those who repented of their sins. She professed before the world her faith in the despised Nazarene, though she well knew that to do so was to expose herself to reproaches, to persecution, and probably to death.

Her splendid mansion became a house of abode to weary and persecuted pilgrims; her immense wealth was devoted to their relief. The poorest of the flock—the poverty-stricken and foot-sore beggar—coming up the great avenue to the door, was met as the father met his prodigal son. She ran out hastily to meet him, took him warmly by the hand and welcomed him. She led him to the best apartment, refreshed him with the choicest wine, supplied him with wholesome food, cheered and clothed her guest, nor suffered him to depart until he was strengthened for his perilous journey.

Throughout all the country her name was famous as the philanthropic, the benevolent, and the affectionate Electa. During this time, and while she was preparing for a better world, and for a fate which, though protracted, was eventually to come upon her, a fearful persecution began, and any one who confessed the name of Jesus was required to recant and deny his faith, or suffer the penalty of the law then promulgated through the country.

Electa was visited by a band of Roman soldiers, whose chief officer proposed the test of "casting a cross on the ground and putting her foot upon it," whereupon he would report her recantation, and she be saved from a painful and ignominious death. She refused, and her family were cast into a dungeon and kept there one year. Then the Roman judge, who had often partaken of her hospitality, and who was anxious to befriend her, came and offered her another opportunity to recant, promising that, if she would do so, she should be protected. Again she refused, and this brought the drama to a speedy close. The whole family, with thousands of others, were put to a cruel death. While she was expiring, and about to pass "to the better land," she prayed with her dying breath: "Father, forgive them, for they know not what they do!"

The sign of the degree is (9).

The pass is (10).

The color appropriate to the degree is RED, which symbolizes fervency, and alludes to the noble generosity of Electa displayed toward the poor, and persecuted of her faith.

The emblem is the CUP, which reminds us of the generous hospitality of Electa, excited by the view of poverty and distress.

The Candidate is conducted around the point of Esther, through the labyrinth to the East, during which the following Ode may be sung. It will be noted that in winding the labyrinth a perfect star has been completed in the marching.

120   ADOPTIVE RITE RITUAL

△

W. PATRON

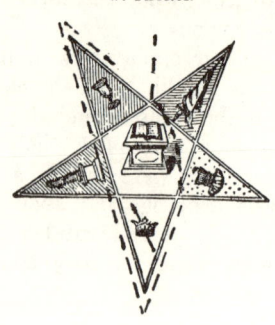

TRIBUTE TO ELECTA

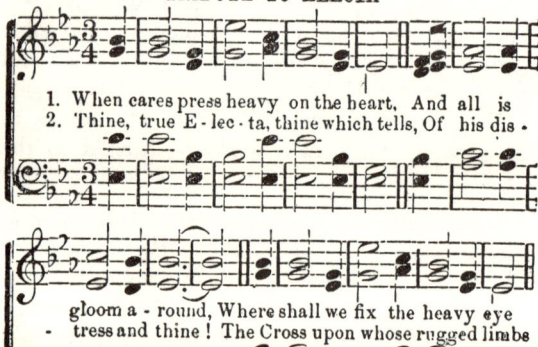

1. When cares press heavy on the heart, And all is
2. Thine, true E-lec-ta, thine which tells, Of his dis-

gloom a-round, Where shall we fix the heavy eye
-tress and thine! The Cross upon whose rugged limbs

In all this mortal bound? What emblem hath the mourner here? What love to warm, what light to cheer?
Ye both did bleed and pine! The Cross by heavenly wisdom given To raise our thoughts from earth to heaven.

COND.—Worthy Patron, again I introduce to you Sister (*naming her*), who has, according to your request, passed through the labyrinth and to the several points of our bright Star, where she has been taught those truly sublime virtues exemplified in the lives of Adah, Jephthah's Daughter, Ruth, Esther, Martha and Electa. You will please further enlighten her by portraying a more complete knowledge of the ceremonies and beauties of our Order.

W. P.—We hail with true pleasure your coming among us. The great work in which we are engaged is amply sufficient for us all, and we shall rejoice to find you excelling in your zeal that of the most devoted members of our society. You will now give attention to the remarks of our Worthy Matron.

W. M.—My dear Sister, for by that endearing title you will hereafter be known among us, in behalf of ...... Chapter, I cordially welcome you to a participation of our privileges.

We are laboring to increase our own happiness and to promote that of others. Our experience and the wisdom we gain from the Scriptures alike, teach us that this world is a harsh, unfriendly scene, poorly adapted to impart felicity; and that it is chiefly by combining the efforts of the good and true, in the work of morality and religion, that happiness is to be acquired and extended.

The greater our ability to do good, the more pleasure we shall enjoy.

We meet *in private*, that we may arrange our plans for the good work in which we are engaged without interruption from those who cannot understand or sympathize with us. In our meetings we strive to learn our duty as beings who possess an immortal part and, when we return home and before the world, it should be our earnest care to perform it. We cultivate a spirit of harmony that the enemy of souls may acquire no advantage over us. And as a large portion of our work lies in acquiring a knowledge of how best to practice the great moral principles,—brotherly love, relief and truth, and in endeavoring to find the true path that leads to everlasting life, we often unite to address the Heavenly Throne and to plead with God that the very spirit of faith and wisdom may descend upon us and make our meeting-place a place like Heaven. In such a prayer let us now, with our Worthy Patron, cheerfully join.

The Patron gives three raps with the gavel ***. *All rise and form a circle around the Altar joining hands. Conductress and Worthy Matron will have the Candidate(s) between them. When the words "golden chain thus lengthened" in the prayer are being pronounced, the W. M. will extend her left hand and take the right hand of the Candidate, and the Conductress will join the circle by taking the Candidate's left hand, thus making the circle complete. When the words "link shall fall away in death" are pronounced in the prayer, the hands shall be unclasped and dropped. At the conclusion of the prayer, the W. P. shall step back into the circle while the Ode is sung.*

PRAYER

W. P.—Source of all Wisdom, Truth and Love! Grant to us that, in the reception of this person, we may add strength to our strength and grace to our grace. Oh, may the golden chain thus lengthened become the brighter for this link, and be strengthened for the great work we do. Enlarge our powers to benefit mankind and to honor God. And when, one by one, each link shall fall away in death, may the parting be temporary and the meeting eternal. In the world where death comes not, may we realize the full happiness of loving and serving Thee forever. Amen.

ODE

Oh! Thou to whom this heart ne'er yet
Turn'd in anguish or regret,
The past forgive, the future spare;
   Sweet Spirit, hear my pray'r.
Oh! leave me not alone in grief,
Send this blighted heart relief;
Send this blighted heart relief.
Make thou my life thy future care,
   Sweet Spirit, hear my pray'r.
Ah! make my life thy future care,
   Sweet Spirit, hear my pray'r;
   Hear, oh! hear my pray'r;
   Ah! hear my prayer.

At the conclusion of the singing, the Patron returns to the East, and seats the Chapter. ° *The Conductress escorts the Candidate to a seat near the East where she will be able to see the Signet and be further instructed by the Patron as follows:*

LECTURE TO THE CANDIDATE

W. P.—My Sister, in taking upon yourself the solemn vows of our Order, you enter upon a new phase of life; you will henceforth be numbered among this beautiful Sisterhood, who have for their inspiration the Star of Bethlehem, which will guide all the faithful to the New Jerusalem—that city not made with hands.

I must remind you that with the privileges come the responsibilities. You have been informed that we are associated together that we may comfort, aid, and protect each other in this our earthly pilgrimage; that our duties to each other are simply labors of love. The covenant of adoption has been rehearsed for you, which you have promised faithfully to keep.

The responsibilities of the Order, therefore, rest lightly upon the faithful, and we trust that you will bear them with that meekness and grace which is found only with the good and true.

You were informed when you first entered this Chapter room that we were in possession of certain secrets, by means of which we were enabled to recognize each other wherever we might meet, and that we propose to put you in possession of these secrets, that you, too, might be recognized as a member of the Order. You have already been conducted to the several points of the Star, where you have received instructions as promised. The signs and passes spoken of were then explained, which, if properly understood, will enable you to make yourself known as a member.

There are five degrees in this Order, which all initiates receive: The first, that of *Adah, the Daughter's;* second, that of *Ruth, the Widow's;* third, that of *Esther, the Wife's;* fourth, that of *Martha, the Sister's;* fifth, that of *Electa, the Mother's.* On undergoing an examination, you will be required to give certain answers to particular questions, and these questions will be asked in the order the degrees were received by you. That you may comprehend the whole work of examination, I will, with the assistance of our Conductress,[1] now rehearse it. You will carefully observe my questions and her answers, as they would be your answers were you undergoing an examination.

W. P.—Sister Conductress, are you a member of the Order of the Eastern Star?

COND.—I ...... (11)

W. P.—What ...? (12)

COND.—I . . . (13)

W. P.—What evidence can you give to prove yourself a member of the Order of the Eastern Star?

COND.—I (14) have . . . signs, ... passes, and .. mottoes, one a general, the other a special ....., a ...., and a ....

W. P.—Please give the signs and passes, and explain them.

---

[1] *This work may be done with the W. Matron or the Conductress, but the latter is preferable. See syllabus for (11), etc.*

COND.—The first is that of Adah; it is given in this manner. (*Gives sign.*)

The pass is *(2).* The Color is blue, represented in the formation of our emblematical star by the violet.

The second is that of Ruth, given in this manner. (*Gives sign.*)

The pass is *(4).* The Color is yellow, represented by the yellow jasmine.

The third is that of Esther, given in this manner. (*Gives sign.*)

The pass is *(6).* The Color is white, represented by the white lily.

The fourth is that of Martha, given in this manner. (*Gives sign.*)

The pass is *(8).* The Color is green, represented by the pine leaf.

The fifth is that of Electa, given in this manner. (*Gives sign.*)

The pass is *(10).* The Color is red, represented by the red rose.

The sixth is the sign of salutation, and is given by a member entering or retiring from a Chapter while at work. Members giving this sign should advance between the altar and Associate Matron, and *(15),* make a slight bow, retire, or take their seats, as the case may require.

W. P.—What is the general motto?
COND.—We * (16).*

ADOPTIVE RITE RITUAL

W. P.—What is the special motto?

COND.—*(17).*

W. P.—Whence did this special motto take its rise?

COND.—From the five heroines of the Order—Adah, because she freely sacrificed her life to save her father's honor.

Ruth, because she willingly left home and friends, to dwell with the people of God.

Esther, because she was prepared to render up her crown, and even life itself, to save her people from destruction.

Martha, from her undeviating faith in the power and merits of her Redeemer.

Electa, because she preferred to suffer death rather than deny her religious belief. These were *(17).*

W. P.—To what word did you refer?

COND.—The cabalistic word, which in an examination should be alternated, I commencing with F (18).* FATAL

W. P.—A., etc., etc.

W. P.—Explain and show our Candidate how Grand Honors are given.

COND.—(19). Right hand over left Bow

COND.—This, Worthy Patron, is all I have to offer, except the grip.

W. P.—Which you will now give to the candidate. (20).

INITIATION

The Patron, addressing the candidate, will say:

W. P.—This, my Sister, completes the work, with the exception of the explanation of the signet. The cabalistic word is so called from its relation to the star; its place is always on the block, forming the base of the star. It is a chain word, holding and binding together the five points of our emblematic star. (*The Patron will point to the signet.*) Its position on the signet is important, as it forms a part of the lesson of examination.

This concludes the ceremonies of initiation. You will now be conducted to the Secretary's desk, where you will sign the by-laws, and then be reconducted to your present position.

The Conductress leads the candidate to the Secretary's desk, where she signs the by-laws, and returns with her to the East. The Chapter is called *** up by the Patron, who says:

W. P.—The candidate will face the West. Sisters and Brothers, of .... Chapter, No. ..., our worthy Sister has passed through the several degrees of our Order, we hope with some pleasure to herself, we know with great satisfaction to us. You will, therefore, give her a hearty welcome.

The Patron hands the gavel to the Matron and resumes his station.

W. M.—Sister Associate Matron.

A. M.—Worthy Matron?

W. M.—You will call the Chapter to recreation, to resume order at the sound of the gavel in the East.

A. M.—Sisters and Brothers, by order of the Worthy Matron, you will now be at recreation, to resume order at the sound of the gavel in the East.

The Conductress or the W. Matron will introduce the candidate to the members, who should receive her kindly, with words of welcome, etc. After which, the W. Matron will call the Chapter to order, proceed with the ordinary business, and finally close the Chapter in form.

The door should be carefully tiled during recreation to prevent the intrusion of improper persons.

INITIATION OF A MASTER MASON

A gentleman, known to be a Master Mason, having been proposed and unanimously elected in a Chapter, presents himself in the preparation room. The order "Initiation" having been reached, the W. Matron will say:

W. M.—Sister Associate Conductress, you will retire and ascertain if there are any candidates in waiting, and report to the Worthy Patron.

W. M. hands the gavel to the Patron who takes charge of the Chapter.

The A. C. retires, and finding a gentleman candidate in the ante-room, ascertains his name, returns to the Chapter room, and says:

A. C.—Worthy Patron, I find in waiting Mr. (*naming the person*), who is, I am informed, a Master Mason, and therefore entitled to receive the light and knowledge of our Order.

W. P.—Sister Secretary, has the petition of Bro. .... been received in open Chapter, and has he been elected?

SEC.—He has.

W. P.—Sister Associate Conductress, you will again retire and introduce the candidate, first giving the usual alarm at the door of the preparation room.

*The A. C. retires, receives the candidate, and gives ***** at the inner door. The Cond., rising in her station, says:*

COND.—Worthy Patron, there is an alarm at the door of the preparation room.

W. P.—Sister Conductress, ascertain the cause of the alarm.

*The Cond. goes to the door, gives *****, opens the door and says:*

COND.—Who knocks at the door of our Chapter?

A. C.—The Associate Conductress, with a candidate, who is desirous of receiving the light and knowledge of our Order.

COND.—(*To the candidate*) Are you willing to assume our obligation of secrecy, and faithfully to perform the duties imposed by the laws of our Order?

CANDIDATE—I am.

COND.—You will wait until the Worthy Patron is informed of your request.

Cond., closing the door, says to the Patron:

COND.—Worthy Patron, the alarm was made by the Associate Conductress, with a candidate who is desirous of receiving the light and knowledge of our Order.

INITIATION OF A MASTER MASON

W. P.—Has he answered the necessary questions?

COND.—He has.

W. P.—Admit him.

Cond. opens the door and says:

COND.—It is the order of the Worthy Patron that this candidate be admitted.

As the Candidate enters, the Conductress leads him to the West and says:

COND.—Sister Associate Matron, I have the pleasure of introducing Mr. ...., to be presented by you to the Worthy Patron. He is desirous of receiving the light and knowledge of our Order, and will pledge his honor in our obligation of secrecy.

A. M.—My friend, you are heartily welcome. Cause the candidate to face the East.

He is placed near the star, facing the East, when the A. Matron will say:

A. M.—Worthy Patron, I have the honor of presenting to you Mr. ......, whose petition has been accepted by this Chapter, and who is desirous of receiving the light and knowledge of our Order.

W. P.—Brother ......, it is with pleasure that

I welcome you into the Order, and especially as a member of this Chapter. The grand purposes of the Order are beneficent and social; its lessons are scriptural; its teachings are moral; its obligations are mutual to all its members, and are based upon the universal principle that, whatever benefits are due by the Masonic Fraternity *to* the wives, mothers, widows, daughters and sisters of Masons, corresponding benefits are due *from* them *to* the Brotherhood. To enable us to properly apply these purposes to the best advantage, we make use of certain signs and ceremonies, by means of which we recognize those who belong to and have a just claim upon us, and mutually bind ourselves by an obligation, not only to secrecy, but to the faithful performance of the duties that devolve upon us as members of this Order.

With this knowledge of its aims and purposes, are you willing to assume the obligations and responsibilities appertaining to this Order?

CANDIDATE—I am.

The candidate answers, and, if in the affirmative, the Patron calls up the Chapter ***, and repeats the obligation, to which the candidate assents. The Patron returns to the dais and seats the Chapter *. If the candidate has never received the signs, passes, etc., he may be brought to the East, and instructed. When time will permit, the following may be rehearsed as a

INITIATION OF A MASTER MASON

CHARGE TO THE CANDIDATE

My Brother, I congratulate you on being found worthy to become a member of this respectable association.

When, in the vicissitudes of life, we are called upon to assume new and untried duties, a sense of responsibility comes over our minds. We ask ourselves, "How far do these new obligations lead us? Why have we taken them? In what way will they contribute to our own happiness, and to the good of those around us?" It shall be my pleasant duty now to answer these questions so far as the Eastern Star may lead us.

The Order of the Eastern Star has no purpose or design save that of promoting happiness. Its secrets are devised only that, by their aid, we may have additional means of distinguishing the *good and true*. Its *source* is the ever-flowing spring of revealed truth. Its *heroines* are selected from the best of those described in the inspired volume. Its *colors* suggest nothing but the purest thoughts. Its *emblems* are borrowed from those that in Scripture foreshadow the life and the house of Almighty God.

Where in human history will you find five female characters so worthy to be combined into *a Star*, as Jephthah's daughter, Ruth, Esther, Martha, and Electa? Can we look for greater excellence, more heroic virtues, or deeds of higher renown, than those that make up the narrative of their lives?

Adah, daughter of Jephthah, loved her father with so great a love, that she gave her young life a ransom for his spotless fame. Ruth, animated by spiritual zeal, left all earthly joys, that she might share the companionship of saints upon earth. Esther rejected the vanities and pride of a royal estate to rescue her people from the hand of the slayer. Martha saw through the cloud of death the assurance of the resurrection, and meekly accepted the promise of her Divine Friend. Electa, summing up the merits and heroism of all the five, yielded her body to the cross, that she might give evidence that she was the child of God. And now the wisest, purest, noblest of womankind may accept these five characters as models of all that women can be in this life and in the life to come.

The affecting and perfect narrations are made graceful by *colors* that both delight the eye and inform the sense. The *Blue*, consecrated to Jephthah's daughter, takes its tinge from the cerulean sky, under which the mountain maid spent the days of her happy youth.

The *Yellow*, consecrated to Ruth, borrows its golden tint equally from the glaring sun above and the ripened corn below, between which throbbed the faithful heart of that matchless damsel of Moab.

The *White*, consecrated to Esther, suggests the dignity which the heroic queen so cheerfully laid aside to preserve the Jewish race from extinction.

The *Green*, consecrated to Martha, leads the chastened spirit through and beyond the grave to all that is animating in the thought of a bright resurrection.

The *Red*, consecrated to Electa, suggests the hospitality inculcated in all the teachings of our Order.

Now, blend these five colors into one; embody them through leaf, and bud, and blossom, in a bright bouquet of flowers; let them flash forth in precious stones and

INITIATION OF A MASTER MASON

enamel; display them in the beautiful regalia of the Order, and this world does not produce anything better calculated to attract and instruct the intelligent mind.

Sisters and Brothers, the vows you have taken are only those whose keeping will make you wiser, better and happier. Our chains are wreathed with flowers. Our duties are sweetened by love. Over us all there hangs the great reward promised by Him whose Star in the East we have seen and Whom we have come to worship.

My Brother, you will now sign the by-laws of this Chapter, which entitles you to full membership, with all the benefits thereof, and subject to all its penalties.

AFFILIATION CEREMONY

The ceremony of affiliation may follow the Star Degrees or take place at any meeting of the Chapter under the order of New Business. The Affiliate must, however, have been balloted on at a Regular meeting.

NOTE: *The affiliation fee must be paid before the affiliation ceremony.*

W. M.—Worthy Patron, I present you the gavel for the affiliation ceremony.

Patron takes the gavel and charge of the Chapter.

W. P.—Sister Conductress, present the Affiliate-elect.

Cond. escorts affiliate to the East at the foot of dais.

COND.—Worthy Patron, I take pleasure in presenting Sister ...., the Affiliate-elect.

W. P.—Sister ...., your petition for affiliation in ...... Chapter has been favorably received and you have been duly elected to receive membership. I present you to our Worthy Matron.

W. M.—My Sister, your standing in the Order of the Eastern Star commends you for adoption to membership in this Chapter. May this alliance

AFFILIATION CEREMONY

benefit you and us in furthering the good work we endeavor to do. On behalf of ...... Chapter, I bid you a cordial welcome. (*W. M. gives a cordial handshake*)

W. P.—Sister Conductress, escort our Sister to the Secretary's desk where she will sign the By-laws and then again present her at the foot of the dais.

Cond. complies with the order.

COND.—Worthy Patron, your order has been obeyed and Sister .... has signed our By-laws.

W. P.—Sister Conductress, cause our new member to face the West.

*Cond. complies and Patron calls up the Chapter with ***.*

W. P.—Sisters and Brothers of ...... Chapter No. ...., and visitors, with great pleasure I present to you Sister .... who has been united with us. You will give her a hearty welcome.

W. P.—Sister Conductress, escort our new member to a seat.

*W. P. then seats the Chapter with * and returns gavel to Matron.*

QUEEN OF THE SOUTH

A DEGREE IN THE SYSTEM OF THE ADOPTIVE RITE AS CONFERRED IN A CHAPTER OF THE EASTERN STAR

This degree, one of the series of the Adoptive Rite, is distinguished as a compliment to all worthy active members of a Chapter of the Order of the Eastern Star.

The degree should be conferred within the Chapter room of the Eastern Star.

An organization of this degree is styled a PALACE. It consists of fourteen officers, and as many members, ladies and gentlemen, as may be convenient.

The officers and stations are:

1. KING SOLOMON (Patron), in the East.

QUEEN OF THE SOUTH 141

2. QUEEN BATHSHEBA (Matron), on the right of Solomon.

3. PRINCESS HATTIPHA (Assistant Matron), in the West.

4. PRINCESS OZIEL (Conductress), in the South.

5. PRINCESS ZORAH (Assistant Conductress), in the North.

6. MYRA (Treasurer), in the Northeast.
7. LEAH (Secretary), in the Southeast.
8. PRINCESS HAGAR (Adah).
9. PRINCESS ORPAH (Ruth).
10. PRINCESS SYENE (Esther).
11. PRINCESS THARAH (Martha).
12. PRINCESS ELLAH (Electa).
13. WARDER, at the door, inside.
14. SENTINEL, at the door, outside.

QUEEN OF SHEBA (Candidate), in front of Solomon in the East.

OPENING CEREMONIES

At the appointed hour of meeting, King Solomon takes his station in the East, and calls the Palace to order °.

SOLOMON—Princess Oziel, proceed to satisfy yourself that all who are within the audience-chamber are entitled to be present.

After taking an observation of all present to assure herself of the truth:

OZIEL—All who are now within the audience-chamber of the Palace are entitled to be present, Most Excellent King Solomon.

SOLOMON—Princess Zorah, communicate with the Warder, and command her vigilance to guard this Palace, and preserve our deliberations from intrusion.

After obeying the order:

ZORAH—Your commands have been obeyed, Most Excellent King Solomon.

SOLOMON—Queen Bathsheba, what are the duties of your station?

BATHSHEBA—To intercede for the Queen of Sheba, and so secure to her a grant of your royal favor.

SOLOMON—Princess Hattipha, what are the duties of your station?

HATTIPHA—To assist in welcoming the Queen of Sheba, and to intercede in her behalf for your royal favor.

SOLOMON—Princess Oziel, what are the duties of your station?

OZIEL—To see that the Palace is in proper order for the reception of visitors; to receive and introduce the Queen of the South to the Most Excellent King Solomon.

SOLOMON—Princess Zorah, what are the duties of your Station?

ZORAH—To see that the Palace is in proper order for the reception of visitors; to assist in receiving and introducing the Queen of the South to the Most Excellent King Solomon.

SOLOMON—Sister Myra, what are the duties of your station?

MYRA—To receive and deposit in the royal treasury all gifts and offerings made to the Most Excellent King Solomon.

SOLOMON—Sister Leah, what are the duties of your station?

LEAH—To make up the records of the royal wisdom, and preserve them in the archives of the kingdom.

SOLOMON—This concourse of duties being performed, make up the system of this degree. In the spirit that should actuate every human being before entering upon any important undertaking, we will invoke a blessing from the Throne of Grace. With our respected Queen Bathsheba, let us pray. *** (*Calls up the Palace*)

PRAYER

BATHSHEBA—Oh, Thou Who art ever ready to hear prayer, and unto Whom all must come in supplication, may we learn at this time to fulfill the royal law of love, and all things whatsoever we would that others should do unto us, may we do even so unto them, remembering that this is the law and the prophets.

Oh, Lord, our Heavenly Father! help us to dismiss all anxious thoughts for the morrow, and to be passive in Thy hands, whether Thou chasten or gladden us, whether prosperity or adversity be ours. Bring us nearer to Thee. Give anything but Thy displeasure, and when our earthly labors are ended, have us with Thyself in that glory which shall be our best and highest reward. Amen.

SOLOMON * —(*seats the Palace*) Sisters and Brothers, there are many thrilling incidents recorded in the Scriptures of the Old and New Testaments, which are embodied in the Degrees of the Masonic Order, much to the pleasure and instruction of the Craft, and of the ladies who share in our privileges. This one concerning Sheba is one of that class, and as there are worthy applicants for the light and benefits of that degree waiting, I therefore declare this Palace duly open for the despatch of such business as may regularly come before it. Sister Warder, you will so inform the Sentinel.

She does so, and says:

WARDER—Your order has been obeyed, Most Excellent King Solomon.

WORKING THE DEGREE

SOLOMON—With the help of the officers I will now proceed to confer the degree known as the Queen of the South.

It was the custom of the great and wise King Solomon to devote one day in the week to public audiences. The renown of this monarch had extended throughout the civilized world, and the greatest Kings and Rulers deemed themselves honored in the title of "Friends of Solomon." Wise men, philosophers, artists, mathematicians, mechanics, all who were skilled in hand, or of bright intelligence, paid their court at the foot of Solomon's throne. Ambassadors from foreign lands, distant and near, came with long and imposing retinues to do him honor. Questions in law, in science, and in religion were confidently propounded to him as to a man from whom nothing had been hidden, to whom nothing was too difficult; and the most intricate problems were solved by him with a readiness that showed the enlightenment he had received from Jehovah.

The degree commemorates one of those audience days, and the visit of the Queen of Sheba, as referred to in the Holy Scriptures.

King Solomon is supposed to be in his Royal Palace, on Mount Zion, seated upon his great throne of ivory, overlaid with pure gold, surrounded with his officers and courtiers, and the kings of foreign nations, ambassadors, philosophers, and others who had come to gather wisdom from his lips.

Oziel, having obtained a list of the candidates, will say:

OZIEL—Most Excellent King Solomon, there are in waiting certain lady relatives of Master Masons, members of the Order of the Eastern Star, accompanied by brethren who are known among us as Master Masons.[1]

These crave the privilege of entering our Palace and receiving the divine precepts, that were anciently communicated to the Queen of the South, from the lips of King Solomon. They are willing to pledge their sacred honor to observe all the lawful rules and regulations of this degree, and I trust that you will grant them an entrance.

The list is handed to the Secretary, who reads it aloud.

SOLOMON—If there are no objections, Sister Warder, you will, at the proper time, instruct the Sentinel to admit the persons named in this list.

In strictness, but one lady candidate should receive this degree at a time. If, however, Solomon sc

---

[1] When there are no gentlemen present the language must be changed accordingly.

chooses, all the lady candidates except one can enter and take their seats, or all enter at the same time, and so receive the degree by communication. The gentlemen candidates invariably receive the degree without ceremony, and all at one inculcation.

SOLOMON—Princess Oziel, you will take a suitable escort, proceed to the outer portals of the Palace, where, I am informed, you will find in waiting the Queen of the South with her retinue. You will welcome and conduct them to our presence in the name of the King of Israel.

Princess Oziel, Zorah, Hagar, Orpah, Syene, Tharah, and Ellah retire to the ante-room. In the meantime, the lady who has been selected as the candidate —representing the Queen of the South—should be dressed in white, with a crown on her head, and a flowing veil attached thereto. A procession is formed and the Candidate placed in the center of the group, Oziel and Zorah leading. As they enter the room, the Palace is called up ***. All remain standing during the introduction; soft music playing.

OZIEL—(*with baton and scroll*) Most Excellent King Solomon, we present before you a noble Princess, Sheba, the Queen of the South, who has entrusted to my hands this written petition.[1]

SOLOMON—Let it be read by Leah, our Secretary.

---

[1] *The petition should be written on a piece of parchment or paper.*

(Taken from the 1894 edition of *Rite of Adoption*)

The scroll is handed to Leah, who reads:

LEAH—"Sheba, the Queen of the South, having heard of the fame of King Solomon, has come from the uttermost parts of the earth to Jerusalem to prove him with hard questions for her own ears must hear the man unto whom God has given the wise and understanding heart. She has brought, in her retinue, a large company with camels bearing spices and pure gold in abundance and precious stones. She beseeches the favor of King

Solomon that she may approach the throne of the King of Israel and make known to him her wishes."

SOLOMON—Never, during the long reign of my father, King David, nor in my own reign, has such a request as this been made to me by a woman. Nevertheless, the Queen of Sheba shall not be denied. Let her make her wishes known.

ZORAH—Most Excellent King Solomon, I present to your royal favor a mighty Princess, Sheba, the Queen of the South, to whom you have granted this audience.

SOLOMON—Mighty Princess, we salute you. (*All salute.*) Be seated. *

The Queen sits directly in front of the King. The officers resume their stations. The Palace is called to order.

SOLOMON—Mighty Queen of Sheba, the Court of King Solomon is open as well to the humblest as to the mightiest. Welcome to the Royal Audience Chamber. Admitted agreeably to your request, I ask you, therefore, to what intent you have approached us this day.

HAGAR—Most Excellent King Solomon, by your gracious permission, I will address you as one of the proxies of the mighty Princess. From the uttermost parts of the earth, oh King Solomon, the Queen of the South has come to Jerusalem to hear thy wisdom and to prove thee with hard questions. Thy fame concerning the name of the Lord has gone forth into every land. From that memorable night, when the Lord appeared unto thee on Gideon, and said, "Ask what I shall give thee," it hath pleased the Most High to grant thee wisdom exceeding much the largeness of heart, even as the sand that is on the seashore. Wiser than all the children of the Eastern country, and all the wisdom of Egypt, God hath made thee wiser than all men, and thy fame is in all nations round about. The representatives of all the people of the earth come to hear thy wisdom, oh Solomon, for all the Kings of the earth have heard thereof. These things having been made known to me by my counselors, it hath seemed good to me, therefore, a woman called, like thyself, to reign over a great people, and feeling greatly the need of Divine wisdom to rule them aright, it hath seemed good unto me, I say, to entreat the King for a share of what God hath so freely dispensed to thee. Therefore, I have crossed lofty mountains, overwhelming rivers, and trackless deserts, by a journey of many months, to seek from thy lips the wisdom granted by the Most High God, and concealed hitherto from the children of men. Let the prayer of my petition then, oh King, come before thee, and refuse me nothing of my request.

SOLOMON—Mighty Princess, while I admire the zeal which hath brought thee so far, and the great and commanding motives that have prompted thee to undertake so painful a pilgrimage, yet, for all that, thy request cannot be granted thee. For look! read in all the records of God's dealings with men, and you will find no instance where it was given to a *woman* to enter into the counsels of the Most High God.

ORPAH—Most Excellent King Solomon, let me also speak as the proxy of this mighty Princess. Consider my request more seriously. When thy royal father, David, sat in his chamber, old and stricken in years, and a conspiracy was formed among his mighty men to make thy elder brother king, thy mother, Bathsheba, went wisely to King David, represented boldly the imminent danger of the occasion and, by her womanly tact and sound judgment, secured the crown of Israel for you. Is not this, then, a striking instance wherein it was given to a woman to penetrate the purposes of the Most High God?

Again, when the two Hebrew mothers stood up before thee, in this audience-chamber, the one with the living child, the other with the dead, they wrought upon thee to display that Divine Wisdom never before vouchsafed to man. Let the prayer of my petition then, oh King, come before thee, and refuse me nothing of my request.

OZIEL—Oh King, the woman hath spoken well. She is worthy, and that her petition be granted, I add my request to hers.

SOLOMON—Mighty Princess, and you, Princess Oziel, truly you have spoken well. Were there no other objection than the one I advanced, you have removed it. But it does not become me, the King of God's chosen people, to establish a precedent in a matter so delicate as this. There is not an example in all history to justify me in granting your request, however strongly you may urge it.

SYENE—Most Excellent King Solomon, let me also speak in behalf of this mighty Queen. Consider her request. It has been proved already that the Most High God has more than once spoken by the mouth of woman in promulgating His decrees.

Let me further name to you Miriam, the sister of Moses, whose counsel was so useful to him both as lawgiver and ruler; and Deborah, the prophetess, who, from her dwelling place under the palm-tree, went forth to counsel and exhort Barak, Israel's great captain, to the salvation of the people; and Jael, the wife of Heber, the Kenite, who, at one stroke, rid her country of its most despotic foe; and others of the brilliant galaxy among the women of Israel. In so many instances has Infinite Wisdom wrought at the hands of woman, that there is ample justification for the wisest of earthly monarchs to set the precedent in this matter and acknowledge her claims at last. Then, oh King, let the prayer of my petition come before thee, and refuse me nothing of my request.

ZORAH—Oh mighty King, the woman hath spoken wisely. She is worthy, and that her petition be granted, I add my request to hers.

SOLOMON—Mighty Princess, and you, Princess Zorah, there is another objection fatal to the gratification of your wishes. It is the want of needful prudence and reticence in your sex. The knowledge vouchsafed to me from the Most High was communicated *secretly,* in the watches of the night, even as Jehovah made known to Samuel the Divine Will at midnight in the Tabernacle at Shiloh. Shall I expose this hidden wisdom to become the subject of gossip, an idle tale to idle tongue? No; a woman cannot keep a secret.

THARAH—Most Excellent King Solomon, you entertain too low an estimate of our sex. Be it known to you that in my country, yea, in all countries of which history gives account, woman has ever proved faithful to every trust reposed in her. Treat her as a slave, and she may exhibit the infidelity of a slave; trust to her as your equal and your friend, and the adamantine rock is not more impenetrable to assault than is the sealed casket of a woman's heart.

Is there a person in this royal audience-chamber

who recalls the memory of a faithful mother, a devoted sister, a trusting wife or daughter, that can deny it? Perish, oh King, the foul assertion that you have uttered. Did not Jochebed, the mother of Moses, preserve the secret of his birth for three months, braving the wrath of Pharaoh, and so secured to Israel its greatest Prophet? Recall the fidelity with which your ancestress, Ruth, preserved the secret entrusted to her. Then, oh King, let the prayer of my petition come before thee, and refuse me nothing of my request.

SOLOMON—Mighty Princess, the Creator Himself, Whom we all recognize and adore, hath declared in His revealed law that the woman is the inferior of the man. It cannot be that knowledge of such infinite importance, that Jehovah condescends to communicate it orally to man, should be transferred to another, born in an inferior state.

ELLAH—Most Excellent King Solomon, read again the Inspired Word which your scribes have preserved from the days of Moses. See there that this want of equality to which you allude (and which is made so much the subject of oppression to woman) does not extend to the region of the *mind* and *soul*. God spoke as lovingly to woman as to man. Sinning together, together have they sorrowed, and His most gracious promises were made to the woman.

How can you declare, then, that she is less than

your equal? Have I not been called to the throne of a mighty kingdom by the same voice that called *you?* Who hath made us, then, to differ, that I should not be allowed a measure of the needful wisdom? Is not the woman man's equal in affections? Has she not even more than her share of life's sorrows? Are not her sentiments more acute, her griefs even more keen than his? Then, oh King, let the prayer of my petition come before thee, and refuse me nothing of my request.

SOLOMON—Mighty Princess, every one in this audience-chamber must admire the logic, apt reply, knowledge of history, and the noble defense of woman evinced in your replies. You have plead the cause of your sex so well that the feelings of our hearers are warmly enlisted in your behalf. I candidly admit that you have answered and removed the objections thus far urged.

There is yet one more that I deem *unanswerable.* It is that, for a woman to participate in the counsels of the Most High, never yet entrusted to one of her sex, will not comport with the modesty, the delicacy, and the decorum that sanctify the intercourse between man and woman in all the walks of civilized life.

HATTIPHA—Most Excellent King Solomon, this is but trifling with my request. Have I not declared to you that the Most High has placed a crown upon my head, which I can in no wise wear, save by the grace of Him Who gave it to me. If it is not a breach of decorum that I should be the ruler over men, where the indelicacy of imparting to me the needful light? Hark ye, O, King Solomon, and all ye who hear me, are we not sojourners together in this evil world for a brief day, and then to pass into a common grave? Mother earth will make no inquiry concerning us, whether man or woman, but will resolve us equally into kindred dust. The trumpet of the archangel will be blown alike to summon us, and the right hand of the Omnipotent will alike raise us to stand before Him. It is but the *fear of man,* O, King, that prompts thee to these repeated denials. I accept them, and I will press my suit no further.

I will now go forth to traverse deserts, mountains, and rivers on my return home. And, as I go, I will make it known that King Solomon, the marvel of mankind for wisdom and Divine gift, has refused to enlighten the Queen of the South in the wisdom God has given him, lest he should set an example to the world.

Keep, then, O, King, the wisdom you have. Soon you must pass away as your fathers, and then all that you have, and all that you are, will be as a shadow that disappeareth. The Word of God abideth forever. To that I will direct me. In prayer, in charity, in deeds of mercy, I will seek the wisdom that I vainly hoped to secure at the

Court of Solomon. My prayer and my request shall come before thee no more.

BATHSHEBA—Most Excellent King Solomon, I have listened to this remarkable debate from the beginning. As the Queen Mother, I am free to advise thee that her request be granted. It is the Divine finger that has directed her to your court. A Divine strength has upheld her in all her weary journeyings hither. A Divine wisdom has prompted her in the words she has uttered. Do not turn her away, then, to make known your refusal to the whole world, and thus cast a shadow upon the perfect wisdom God has given thee.

SOLOMON—Sister Secretary, look you into the law of Moses, and into the history of God's people, recorded by the prophet Samuel, and see if there is anything in the treasuries of inspiration that will enlighten us upon the relation between man and woman.

SEC.—God created man in His own image; in the image of God created He him; male and female created He them. The Lord God said, "It is not good that man should be alone; I will make him an helpmeet for him." In all the Divine commands in favor of the poor and distressed, no class of persons is so often and so kindly mentioned as the widow.

Most Excellent King Solomon, the law of Moses everywhere regards the woman equally worthy of God's favor as man, and if she is not so often mentioned in these it is because her lot is more retired. Whenever the writers of Joshua, Judges, Ruth, and Samuel speak of the part performed by woman in the great drama of our nation, it is in the most respectful and reverential terms. The history of the mother of Samson and the mother of Samuel, of Jephthah's daughter, of your own noble ancestress, Ruth, and of many others, affords ample assurance that, in the favor and mercy of God, the woman shares a full portion with the man.

SOLOMON—Look you now, my respected Queen Mother, into the Psalms of my royal father, David, and see if there is anything in the treasuries of inspiration there that will enlighten us upon the relation between man and woman.

BATHSHEBA—Harken unto me, oh my son. Under the guise of a beautiful and virtuous woman, the royal Psalmist prefigures the glories of the Kingdom of Christ. In all the exhibitions of the sins of Israel, and they are many, he nowhere alludes to a dishonorable woman. The mourning for a mother he depicts as the most grievous of earthly sorrows. And so the Psalms of David, your noble father, everywhere regard the woman equally worthy of God's favor with the man. And in almost every instance is *man* used in the generic sense to include *both sexes*.

SOLOMON—Mighty Princess, I can no longer forbear to grant your request. Truly, God *has* sent you here, and you shall now be enlightened. A faithful witness will not lie. Hope deferred maketh the heart sick. The lips of truth shall be established forever. Samson, when tempted by Delilah, revealed to her the secret of the Lord, and, as a punishment, the Lord sent upon him the prison-house, blindness, and death. Saul was stricken to the earth by the machinations of the Witch of Endor, and he went forth from her cave to meet a bloody death.

But you, oh Mighty Princess, who have come so far, not influenced by vain curiosity or the purpose to do evil, or gain unlawful knowledge, you will receive this wisdom that you may apply it to the good of your people. Therefore, I will no longer delay to share it with you. Know then, oh Queen of the South, and you, Sisters and Brothers, who are around me, that the Lord God will do nothing but He revealeth His secrets unto His servants. The secret things belong unto the Lord our God, and there is a God that revealeth secrets. Job declared, "The secret of God was upon my tabernacle, in the days when God preserved me." And David prophesied, "He that dwelleth in the secret place of the Most High shall abide under the shadow of the Almighty."

Do you ask to whom the secrets of the Lord shall be revealed? The law is open to our eyes, "the secret of the Lord is with them that fear Him, and He will show them His covenant." "His secret is with the righteous." But what is this secret wisdom that the wisest have longed to know equally with the fool? Hear ye, oh my friends, and be profited thereby. Fear God and keep His commandments, for this is the whole duty of man. For God shall bring every work into judgment with every secret thing, whether it be good or whether it be evil. THE FEAR OF THE LORD, THAT IS WISDOM, AND TO DEPART FROM EVIL IS UNDERSTANDING.

SOLOMON—Sisters and Brothers, in this beautiful allegory we have considered the objections urged against the admission of ladies into the knowledge of Masonic principles. Those objections advanced by King Solomon were so easily answered and refuted by the Queen of the South, that it was impossible even for the wisest of men to maintain them.

How much more difficult is it in these latter days, when we are educating our daughters equally with our sons, and in this great and enlightened country, where Oriental customs cannot degrade our women into slaves or silly toys, how much more difficult, I say, to maintain an argument against the adoption of ladies into binding and honorable covenants.

I am rejoiced, then, to assure you that although the advice and the influence of unfounded custom may for a little time, and in a few places, exclude ladies from our social and moral privileges, yet, by far the majority of Freemasons are already agreed to share the enjoyments and employments of the Order with the wives, mothers, sisters, and daughters of the Craft, so far as they may lawfully do so. I hail each lady here as a Queen of the South, and will proceed to communicate to you the secrets of the degree.

The Palace is called up. ***

The following—(21)—is then read. Every person present is required to........during the reading of the—(21)—.[1]

Solomon— * (*seats the Palace*)

Solomon—The—(22)—of the degree consist of —(a), the—(b), the—(c), and the—(d). The—(a). The—(b). The—(c); the—(d). The Symbolic—(e).

CHARGE TO THE CANDIDATES

SOLOMON—Sisters and Brothers, the beautiful and instructive legends which form the foundation of this degree have been so elaborately wrought out in the ceremonials, which have been dramatized before you, that any further instruction upon the subject is superfluous. That the female relatives of our Order are entitled to participate with us in the great privileges of Freemasonry is so clear and demonstrable that but few persons in this enlightened age are hardy enough to deny it, and I can

[1] *See syllabus for* (21), *etc.*

assure you that any intelligent lady who will urge her claims persistently and properly, as the Queen of Sheba did, may ask and receive, seek and find, knock and it shall be opened unto her.

(Taken from the 1894 edition of *Rite of Adoption*)

ADDRESS OF THE QUEEN

At the conclusion of the charge, the candidate steps forward two or three paces. Her escort, viz. Oziel, Zorah, Hagar, Orpah, Syene, Tharah and Ellah, form a semi-circle behind her. Bathsheba and Hattipha come from their stations and stand at the right and left of the candidate.

The candidate then repeats the following

TRIBUTE OF GRATITUDE

SHEBA—Most Excellent King Solomon, and you, Gracious Queen Mother, Princesses and Lords, in the distant land where I was born, we are taught that there is but one God, and that He puts it into the hearts of such as He will to speak forth sentiments of wisdom suitable to the guidance of all His creatures. In coming hither from the uttermost parts of the earth, I was actuated by no other desire than to learn the will of the great God of Heaven. What you have told me, Most Excellent King Solomon, is wise and good, and upon my return I will make it my care to teach to others what is the good and acceptable will of God.

Speaking for my sex, O, King Solomon, I declare that we have never sought to go beyond the bounds allotted to us by our Creator. We have cheerfully submitted to endure the ills of life, restricted to a humble and retiring condition, patient to bear our portion according to the will of God. The domestic circle is ours. We claim to rule the fireside. The culture of the infant mind in enstrusted to us, and we do not crave to step beyond our sphere.

But when you—our fathers, brothers, husbands, sons—when you claim to possess a social bond woven by God Himself, and handed down to you through the ages, we have the right to some share in it. When you tell us that the protection, the honor, the sustenance of wife and daughters are involved in these ancient ties, we have the right to possess some means of claiming our share in such inestimable privileges. While we do not ask for a knowledge of the *essential secrets* of Freemasonry, we do feel to demand of our husbands, fathers, brothers, sons, some *tokens* by which we may distinguish a Freemason from a base pretender, and so be enabled to accept or reject him according to his respective merits.

This is all, Most Excellent King Solomon, that we have ever demanded. In the process of time, under the better influences of civilization and a purer religion, the condition of woman has been steadily raised. Our daughters have a glorious prospect in the future for honor and usefulness. If there is anything in Freemasonry, then, planted there by divine inspiration—anything which we are entitled to know, and which is calculated to advance our sex—*let us know it,* and see if we will not prove ourselves worthy of Masonic confidence.

Finally, Most Excellent King Solomon, and you, Gracious Queen Mother, Princesses and Lords, I thank you for the trust you have reposed in me. I speak as the representative of woman, when I say that if you ever have traitors among you who will reveal your secrets and disgrace your confidence, those traitors will not be of my sex.

Inviolably sealed in my heart of hearts, I will

treasure what you have given me this hour, and this tongue shall be torn from its place before the least of your secrets shall be unlawfully made known.

All resume their stations.

CLOSING CEREMONIES

The proceedings being ended, and the records made up and approved, the Palace is thus closed:

SOLOMON—Sister Warder, inform the Sentinel at the utmost precincts of our Palace, that this Palace is about to be closed.

The order is obeyed.

An Ode may be sung, or remarks may be made by persons present.

SOLOMON—I now declare this Palace of King Solomon closed. Sister Warder, you will so inform the Sentinel. *

FORM OF CERTIFICATE FOR QUEEN OF THE SOUTH

This is to Certify that _____ has received the Complimentary Degree of QUEEN OF THE SOUTH having previously received the Five Degrees of the ORDER OF THE EASTERN STAR in _____ Chapter No. ___, located at _____, and working under a Charter from the GRAND CHAPTER OF THE STATE OF _____. In Testimony Whereof, we have granted this CERTIFICATE under our hand and seal this __ day of _____.

(Seal)

Secretary of _____ Chapter No. __

MATRONS' AND PATRONS' ADMINISTRATIVE DEGREE

This degree is designed to be the official complement and guide for those who have been elected or installed as Matrons and Patrons of regularly constituted Chapters of the Eastern Star. It may be conferred on one or more Matrons and Patrons from different Chapters constituted under the same Grand Chapter.

It should be conferred before Installation, or as soon after as possible. Being strictly an official grade, it is intended to inspire, to instruct and to draw into closer bonds of official intimacy those who are about to assume, or have assumed, these high offices.

The degree is conferred by THE ADMINISTRATIVE COUNCIL consisting of not less than three Worthy Patrons, Past Worthy Patrons, Worthy Matrons, or Past Worthy Matrons of the Chapter Order of the Eastern Star (except at the formation of a new Chapter, there being no Past Patrons or Past Matrons); also, by courtesy, the Worshipful Masters and Past Masters of Craft Masonry, and officers of Grand Lodges who are in harmony or affiliation with Chapters of the Eastern Star. But every Freemason, not a Worthy Patron or Past

Worthy Patron, before being admitted as a constituent member of the COUNCIL, must assume a pledge under the sanctity of his Masonic obligation that he will not improperly impart the secrets of this degree, or be instrumental in so doing.

The officers conferring the degree shall be Past Patrons and Past Matrons *who have previously received this degree* insofar as possible. If the required number of such is not obtainable, the unfilled offices may be occupied by such persons as are *qualified* to receive the degree, they being Past Patrons and Past Matrons who have not heretofore had the degree conferred on them. The occupancy of office by such persons shall then be interpreted as conferring the degree on them, they having joined in repeating the obligation during the present ceremony.

It has become customary in many jurisdictions to have the Grand Chapter control this degree and the ADMINISTRATIVE COUNCIL to be composed of Grand Chapter Officers.

The ADMINISTRATIVE COUNCIL is called together in the Chapter room at the summons of the retiring or newly elected Worthy Patron of a Chapter, or by some officer of the Grand Chapter having jurisdiction.

If desired, the HISTORY may be given as part of the ceremony and may be given by the Worthy Patron, or assisted by the Worthy Matron as indicated.

OPENING CEREMONY

When ready for the opening ceremony, the Administrative Council officers acting as Worthy Patron, Worthy Matron (Associate Matron), Secretary, Conductress, Warder and (Sentinel) take their respective stations in the Chapter room. If the Council consists of sufficient number, they may march in as in an Eastern Star Chapter, and follow the same procedure in Opening, using an Associate Conductress, A. M., etc.

SHORT FORM OPENING

W. M.—Sister Warder, you will instruct the Sentinel that we are engaged in the solemn ceremonies of opening the Council and direct him to permit no interruption while we are thus engaged.

Warder obeys and reports.

W. M.—Sister Conductress, are all the Sisters entitled to be present?

COND.—All the Sisters are entitled to be present, Worthy Matron.

W. M.—Worthy Patron, are all the gentlemen entitled to be present?

ADMINISTRATIVE DEGREE

W. P. will ascertain if all gentlemen have been obligated in the degree and, if necessary, take their pledge.

W. P.—All the gentlemen are entitled to be present, Worthy Matron.

W. M.—Sister Conductress, attend at the Altar.

Cond. opens the Bible at the 5th Chap. of JUDGES, *and resumes her station.*

W. M.—I now declare this Administrative Council duly open. *

W. M.—Worthy Patron, we are ready for the conferring of the Administrative Degree. (*hands him the gavel*)

W. P.—Sister Secretary, you will read the names of those who are to receive the Administrative Degree in this Council.

Secretary reads the names.

W. P.—Sister Conductress, you will escort the candidate(s) to a seat near the East.

HISTORY

W. P.—In the distant ages, over 3500 years ago, among the hills of Palestine, dwelt DEBORAH, the prophetess, in a tent under a palm tree. The history of this remarkable woman, although brief, is replete with interest.

W. M.—The people of Israel had fallen into evil in the sight of the Lord and He had sold them into the hand of Jabin, King of Canaan, who reigned in Hazor the captain of whose host was Sisera. He had nine hundred chariots of iron; and twenty years he mightily oppressed the children of Israel.

They spread forth their hands, but there was no one to comfort them. The tears ran down their eyes because the Comforter that should relieve them was far from them. Their children were desolate because the enemy prevailed over them.

To Deborah, the prophetess, the wife of Lapidoth, came the people for counsel and for judgment because she was a woman endowed with superhuman knowledge, prudence, and power, and eminently qualified to rule and govern.

Grieving over the desolation to which her countrymen had been brought for their sins, and believing that their punishment was enough, and that God would be moved to pity and to pardon, she accepted the call of the people, and set about the work of their deliverance. A *"Mother in Israel,"* she sought for a warrior of approved bravery and experience to lead the patriotic hosts to battle. This she found in the person of BARAK the son of Abinoam, a resident of Kedesh of Naphtali, far in the north, and to him announced the will of God, that he should redeem Israel by the power of the sword. She commanded him to make Mount Tabor his rallying-place, with ten thousand of the mountaineers of his own and the neighboring tribes, while she by her wisdom, would draw Sisera, with his chariots and multitude, to the river Kishon, in the plain of Jezreel, and there would deliver them into his hand.

The *Signal Sign* and *Summons* sent from the judgment seat under the palm tree in Mount Ephraim to Kedesh-Naphtali were preserved among the Israelites, and are adopted as a part of the secret instructions of this degree.

W. P.—Barak, although brave and experienced in the mountain warfare of his race, was alarmed at the power and magnitude of the enemy and, under the disheartening feelings of the times, he returned this reply:—"If thou wilt go with me, then I will go; but if thou wilt not go with me, then I will not go."

The *Sign of Refusal* returned through the messenger of Deborah is preserved and adopted as a part of the secret instructions of this degree.

W. M.—Then Deborah arose and went through

the length of the land to the home of Barak. Yet it was with womanly indignation and rebuke that she answered his appeal saying: "I will surely go with thee, notwithstanding the journey that thou takest shall not be for thine honor, for the Lord shall sell Sisera into the hand of a woman."

W. P.—Then Barak collected his forces, ten thousand strong, poorly armed, and weakened by the long and crushing despotisms of their conquerors upon the summit of Mount Tabor, and Deborah went up with him. There, as in a panorama, were spread abroad the innumerable forces of the enemy. For "Sisera had gathered together all his chariots, even nine hundred chariots of iron," and all his people unto the river Kishon.

W. M.—It is no matter of surprise that the small army of Israelites hesitated to engage in war under such tremendous odds. Long slavery weakens both body and mind. Their fruitful fields would be turned into deserts, their cities destroyed, all that was dear to them on earth threatened with slaughter should this sudden rebellion fail, presented an image too terrible for contemplation.

But the indomitable Deborah, putting her trust in God, commanded her hero to lead his forces against the enemy at once. "Up," she cried, "for this is the day in which the Lord hath delivered Sisera into thine hand. Is not the Lord gone out before thee?" So, Barak, in obedience to this imperative command, went out from Mount Tabor, and ten thousand men with him.

The *Command Sign* used by Deborah, is perpetuated and adopted as a part of the secret instructions of this degree.

W. P.—This prediction by Deborah was fulfilled. The "Lord discomfited Sisera, and all his chariots, and all his host, with the edge of the sword before Barak." All fell before the edge of the sword and there was not a man left. Sisera himself, fleeing homeward alone, was slain in the tent of Heber, the Kenite, by the hand of a woman, as Deborah had foretold.

W. M.—The next day saw Deborah at the height of her glory and popularity. She was again seated in council, under her palm tree, surrounded by the princes and nobles of Israel, who gave to her, for superior wisdom and judgment, the honor of freeing Israel from their oppressors. Deborah's heart bounded with joy, but checking all pride, she said, "Not unto me—not to Deborah be the glory, my lords; let us ascribe it all to our merciful Jehovah, of whom I am only the humble instrument."

And the land had rest forty years.

THE WORK OF FAITH

W. P.—This example of Deborah shows what strong faith in a single woman may do for a whole nation. It may possibly do more at the present period in the world's history than ever before. It does not need an appointment to the office of a prophet, nor the exercise of public gifts, nor the commanding genius of a conqueror, but a patient, earnest and persevering spirit of faith and labor to accomplish the good and noble works for which we believe woman in her sphere of life is created.

[Doubtless, the analogy between the administrative association of Deborah and Barak, in Palestine, and that of Matron and Patron in our Chapters, is very evident to you. You have noted that Deborah and Barak inspired and led their people to great endeavor and achievement, and encouraged, counseled, and directed them in their affairs. So, likewise, the Matron and the Patron of a Chapter should inspire their Chapter members to earnest endeavor, lead, encourage and counsel them in the accomplishment of good deeds.]

CHARGE TO MATRON

W. P.—My Sister, you have been thought worthy to occupy the distinguished position of Worthy Matron of a Chapter of the Order of the Eastern Star, and we are assembled for the purpose of investing you with the powers appropriately adapted to assist you to preside over and govern a legally constituted Chapter, and binding you by a special tie to be faithful to duty.

ADMINISTRATIVE DEGREE

It is called the *Administrative Degree*, and is intended to explain and dignify the powers, duties, and responsibilities of the presiding officers of a warranted Chapter of the Eastern Star.

It is necessary that every person eligible and worthy of being elected to the honorable position of Worthy Matron should consider that, since God hath given her an excellent nature, wisdom, and the power to choose between good and evil, an understanding soul, and an immortal spirit, He hath also appointed for her a work and a service great enough to employ those abilities, and hath also designed her to a state of life after this to which she can only arrive by that service and obedience.

To discharge in a proper manner the duties of Worthy Matron is no sinecure; nor is the practice of beneficence a life of ease and indolent contentment. She must not do the work of the Order negligently and idly, but in respecting those who have honored her by their suffrages, and in performing the task allotted to her, she should put forth all her strength, and assist to lighten the burdens and necessities of her sisters.

The progress and advancement of the Order of the Eastern Star will greatly depend upon you and your successors. Out of the fitness to govern alone grows the right to govern. All things of weight and import are to be done with due and grave solemnity, in evidence that we understand the importance of that matter which we have in hand. Solemn ceremonials are not empty pageants or vain shows. All the wise men and all the good men of the world are obedient to their governors, and no person ever came to perfection but by obedience. And so we have chosen such institutions and manners of living in which we may not choose our own work, nor follow our own will, nor entirely please ourselves but, to some degree, be accountable to others, and subject to discipline, and obedient to command. We know that what health is to the body and peace to the spirit, that is government to the societies of the human family.

Therefore, since you have been selected as Worthy Matron of ...... Chapter, No. .., it is much needful that you should be apt and fit to govern and render justice. The proper dispensing of justice is the great interest of humanity on earth. It is the ligament which holds civilized beings and civilized nations together. Wherever her temple stands, and so long as it is duly honored, there is a foundation for social security, general happiness, and the improvement and progress of our race. And whoever labors on this edifice with usefulness and distinction, whoever clears its foundations, strengthens its pillars, adorns its entablatures, or contributes to raise its august dome still higher in the skies, connects himself, in name and fame and character, with that which is and must be as durable as the fame of human society.

The high position to which you have attained in the Order is the best proof that you are acquainted with the requisites necessary to constitute an efficient Matron, and are familiar with the duties and serious responsibilities which will necessarily devolve upon you. The honor, reputation, and usefulness of your Chapter will chiefly depend upon the mode in which you discharge the duties of your office. If you should be satisfied with merely knowing by rote the formulas, the phrases and the ordinary ceremonials of the work, having no care or concern for your Chapter, you *may* maintain good order and conduct the work with regularity, but you will soon see indifference take the place of zeal, inattention to punctuality, lassitude of interest, and immobility of activity.

The Matron of a Chapter ought to possess *knowledge* to diversify her instructions; *judgment* to preserve the happy medium between rashness and timidity; *talent* to address the sisters at length on every emergency; *tact* to conciliate disputes and reconcile contending parties; and *presence of mind* to decide correctly on any sudden indiscretion or irregularity which may occur among the members of the Chapter, that order and good feeling may be perfect and complete. The great secret of government is to understand correctly under what circumstances authority ought to be exercised, and when it should be profitably withheld. She must never exercise partiality, or be detected in the slightest bias in favor of individuals. The sister who possesses *all these qualifications* will rule and govern her Chapter with honor to herself and satisfaction to the sisters; it will represent a well regulated and happy family, where harmony and loving kindness will prevail among the members.

The beacon that should turn all its rays *inward,* and confine them to the narrow precincts which it occupies, would be useless to the mariner feeling his way through storm and darkness toward an unseen haven. The Chapter that gives no light beyond its walls, or the tree that bears no useful fruit, is like the individual who locks up his knowledge in his own bosom, and plays the churl with the treasures that God has loaned him for the common benefit.

You are to arouse the indolent, encourage the despondent, and invite the reflecting sisters to perform some service, the influence of which shall be felt beyond the limits of the Chapter; something for society; something for humanity; something for God. Whenever your Chapter is closed, and a meeting has passed without your having given your associates some inspiration to renewed efforts, the distressed comforted, you will have failed to do your duty. Omit no opportunity to impress upon them the import and weight of those obligations. Comment upon them, over and over, in all their startling solemnity. Continually admonish the sisters of the duty that rests upon them, so to act and behave as to bring no discredit or reproach upon the Order.

We hope that you will, in all respects, and under all circumstances, perform your duty; and that when you lay down the insignia of office your example will remain as the best and brightest of lessons for your successors so that they, too, may win for themselves honor and reputation. May it be said of you, in the words of Holy Writ, "She openeth her mouth with wisdom; and in her tongue is the law of kindness."

CHARGE TO PATRON

W. P.—My Brother, you have been elected by the members of your Chapter to occupy the most exalted position in their power to bestow upon a gentleman, a just compliment to your zeal and worth.

The high honors attached to the office of Worthy Patron are accompanied by weighty and delicate responsibilities. You are not the chief officer, yet, in all things pertaining to the work of the Chapter, your advice and counsel will be sought and the cooperative manner with which you comply, remembering that it is not your province to be dictatorial, will determine the harmony and progress of the Chapter.

You are to preside during the conferring of the degrees and it is your duty to see that the officers are proficient in the rendition of the ritualistic work and that no deviation be made therefrom.

It is your duty to ascertain whether the Master Masons present in the Chapter room are entitled to be there and to obligate them when necessary.

You are expected to have a watchful care over the interests of the Chapter and to see that the laws of the Order are promptly obeyed by the members, but that you will feel called upon to exemplify in your conduct through life the excellent tenets of our Order and so prove, by your good example, that the members have found in you a brother in whom they can perfectly confide, ever remembering your obligations to both the Masonic Fraternity and the Order of the Eastern Star and thereby contribute to furthering the good work in which we are engaged.

You are to assist the Worthy Matron in the discharge of her duties; you are to study the rules and regulations and be proficient in the laws of parliamentary law that you may give timely advice and assistance to the Worthy Matron in the determination of such matters.

Maintain with unswerving care the constitutions and regulations of the Order and, in your respect for law and good government, cause all others to find the strongest incentive of obedience to all lawful commands.

Before the secrets of the degree can be imparted to you, I shall require your solemn pledge of honor.

Sister Conductress, place the Candidate(s) in proper position. * * *

PRAYER

Our Father, who art in Heaven, be present with us in our deliberations. Uphold us with Thy right hand. Guide us in the paths of peace. Endue us with Faith, Hope, and Charity. Enable us to determine with wisdom, to act with firmness, to bear with us patiently, and to pity and forgive all who do us wrong. Amen.

W. P.—*Gives first part of* (23).[1]

You will give your name in full and repeat after me ——(23).

W. P.—* (*seats the Council*) My Sister (*and Brother*), with the assistance of the Conductress, you will now be given the word of, *etc.* (24)

At the end of the explanation, which may be given with the W. M. instead of Cond., the Patron will say:

W. P.—This concludes the degree. ° Sister Conductress, escort our Sister (*and Brother*) to the Secretary's desk and cause her (*them*) to sign her (*their*) name(s) in the records as having received

---
[1] *See Syllabus for* (23), *etc.*

the Administrative Degree on this evening, and then escort her (*them*) to a seat(*s*). (*hands the gavel back to W. M.*)

W. M.—The work of this Council having been completed, we shall proceed to close. Sister Conductress, attend at the Altar. (*done*) Sister Warder, inform the Sentinel that this Council is closed.

If desired, the Patron may offer a prayer before Bible is closed.

W. M.—Farewell.

ALL—Farewell.

W. M.—*

FORM OF CERTIFICATE FOR ADMINISTRATIVE DEGREE

This is to Certify that .... has received the ADMINISTRATIVE DEGREE of the ORDER OF THE EASTERN STAR, having been elected on ...., 19.. to serve as Worthy ..atron in .... Chapter No. ...., O.E.S., located at .... and working under a Charter from the Grand Chapter of the State of .... and that ..he has been properly instructed in the powers, duties, and responsibilities of such office.

In Testimony Whereof we have granted this CERTIFICATE under the hand and seal of the following officers of competent jurisdiction of the ADMINISTRATIVE COUNCIL this .... day of ...., 19...

Attest ....
  Secretary of ...... Chapter   ....
  No. ....

ELECTION OF OFFICERS

The Worthy Patron shall preside during the Election of Officers which shall take place at the *Regular* meeting next preceding December 27 (Festival of St. John, the Evangelist) and Installation should be on the same, or at the next *Regular* meeting.

The *elective* officers of a Chapter are: Worthy Patron, Worthy Matron, Associate Matron, (*Associate Patron*),[1] Treasurer, Secretary, (*Trustees*),[2] Conductress, and Associate Conductress, who shall be elected annually, by ballot, by a majority of the members present.

The *appointed* officers are: Warder, Marshal, (*Musician*), Adah, Ruth, Esther, Martha, Electa, Sentinel, (*Flag Bearers*), and (*Chaplain*), who shall be appointed by the Worthy Matron at the time of her installation.

Compensation, if any, for any officers of the Chapter, shall be approved *before* the election or appointment of such officers.

---

[1] *Officers listed within parenthesis ( ) are optional, depending on the regulation of the Grand Chapter.*
[2] *It is customary to elect one Trustee for 3 years, one for 2 years, and one for 1 year at the first election held for Trustees, and thereafter, one Trustee shall be elected annually for a term of 3 years.*

In event a candidate for office shall not receive a majority of all votes cast, the candidate receiving the lowest number of votes shall be dropped and an additional ballot shall be taken for such office until a majority vote is secured.

A member of the Chapter may be elected to office although absent from the meeting, providing written consent of such member is given, but such officer may not be installed *in absentia.*

Members in arrears of dues for one year, ending December 31st, shall not hold office, nor be entitled to vote for elective officers.

VACANCIES

In case of the death, resignation, absence or other disability of the Worthy Matron to preside, the Associate Matron, of right, will assume the position and responsibilities of the Chair. If both these officers are absent or unable to attend the meetings of the Chapter, the Patron will appoint a Past Matron, in good standing, to preside during their temporary or permanent absence, until the next annual election.

Vacancies in the elective offices may be filled by ballot, at a stated meeting, the members having been duly summoned for that purpose. Vacancies in the appointed offices may be filled by the Worthy Matron at a stated meeting.

ANNUAL INSTALLATION OF OFFICERS OF A SUBORDINATE CHAPTER

Every officer of a subordinate Chapter must be installed before assuming his or her duties.

The objections of a member cannot prevent the installation of an officer who has been regularly elected.

The retiring Worthy Patron, a Past Patron, or a Grand Officer, shall preside at the Installation of Officers, except at the installation of officers of a *new* Chapter, when the Grand Patron, or an authorized Deputy shall do the installing.

The Installing Patron, after assuming the Chair, will request the Worthy Matron to turn over to him the Chapter, By-laws and Constitution, and Gável. He may make a short address of congratulation to the retiring Matron. He will appoint a Sister to act as the Installing Marshal, the retiring Matron preferred, and a Brother as Assistant Installing Marshal. He will request the Chapter officers to vacate their stations, turning over their officers' jewels to the Installing Marshals who will place them on the Altar (or table) for convenience. The Secretary will then read the names of the Officers who are to be installed.

PUBLIC INSTALLATION

Many a worthy Sister or Brother was first inspired to become a member of the Order of the Eastern Star because of an impressive Installation Ceremony which she or he witnessed. Should the Installation Ceremony be open to non-members, great care must be taken to omit such parts of the ceremony as are not proper to be performed in the presence of strangers. On such occasions, the Installing Officer should deliver an address, giving a brief history and explaining the principles and aims of the Order. If the entire meeting is open to non-members, the Opening and Closing Ceremonies should omit all reference to guarding the door, signs, passwords, etc. The officers may enter as in a regular opening and the Worthy Matron, after having been escorted to the East, the other officers assuming their stations, should welcome not only the Sisters and Brothers, but friends as well, with appropriate remarks as:

W. M.—Sisters and Brothers, and friends, on behalf of .... Chapter No. ...., I bid you a cordial welcome. We have assembled at this time for the purpose of installing the officers of this Chapter. By the rules of the Order, this service is permitted to be performed in public, and it is our hope that the exercises may be both pleasing and interesting to all.

INSTALLATION OF OFFICERS

Recital of the officers' duties should be omitted in the opening as these will be given in the Installation of the new officers. The opening ode will be sung and the Conductress will attend at the Altar. The W. M. will turn the gavel over to the Installing Patron who will call up the assembly for prayer.

I. W. P.—*** Our Father, Who art in Heaven, from Whom cometh all wisdom, look upon and bless us in the duties we are about to perform. May these officers who are now to be invested with authority to govern in this Chapter be impressed with the importance of the trusts confided to them. Endue them with wisdom that they may rightly discharge every duty; with love, that they may exemplify the beauty of concord in all their doings; with fidelity, that they may not fail in the performance of every obligation; with fortitude, that they may fearlessly face every obstacle and conquer every difficulty. And grant that peace and harmony may prevail among all the members of this Chapter and the Order. Direct us in the ways of truth and love, and may all be done in Thy holy name. Amen.

WORTHY MATRON

I. W. P.—* Sister Marshal, you will now present the Worthy Matron-elect for installation.

She conducts her in front of the Patron.

I. MAR.—Worthy Patron,[1] it is with great pleasure that I present Sister ...., who has been elected Worthy Matron of this Chapter for the ensuing year. Our Sister is not unmindful of the important responsibility that rests upon her in the acceptance of this trust; yet she is willing to assume it in the hope that, by the aid of her Sisters and Brothers and the favor of God, she will be enabled to properly fulfill the duties of the office, and not prove unworthy of the high honor that has been conferred upon her.

I. W. P.—Sister ...., before proceeding with your investiture, it is necessary that you should signify your assent to those Regulations of the Order, upon the strict observance of which the stability and success of our organization mainly depend.

Do you admit that the Chapter Order of the Eastern Star is the basis of the Adoptive Rite, and that the name, character, and mode of recognition of the Order are unchangeable?

ANS.—I do.

Do you admit that a belief in the existence of a Supreme Being is absolutely necessary to membership in the Order?

ANS.—I do.

Do you promise to protect and obey the laws and

---

[1] *If it be the Grand or Associate Grand Patron, she will address him as Grand Patron.*

INSTALLATION OF OFFICERS

regulations of the Grand Chapter, and the edicts of the Grand Patron, and to permit no violation of them by the members of your Chapter?

ANS.—I do.

Do you agree that the ceremonies of initiation can in no case be conferred, unless a Master Mason, in regular standing, presides?

ANS.—I do.

Do you admit that no new Chapter shall be formed without permission of the Grand Chapter, or Grand Patron; and that no countenance be given to any illegally formed Chapter, its members, or persons initiated therein?

ANS.—I do.

Do you agree that no visitor shall be received into your Chapter without due examination, nor when such visitor is likely to disturb the peace and harmony thereof?

ANS.—I do.

Do you agree that no person can be regularly initiated in or admitted a member of a Chapter without previous notice, and proper investigation as to character?

ANS.—I do.

Do you agree to promote the welfare of this Order, and will use your utmost endeavors to make yourself useful and your station honorable?

ANS.—I do.

Do you promise to support and maintain these

rules and regulations, and to enforce their observance by the members of your Chapter?

ANS.—I do.

I. W. P.—Members of ...... Chapter No. ......, you have heard your Sister-elect in the sacred pledges she has made. Do you still entertain the wish that she should preside over the Chapter the coming year?

MEMBERS—We do.

I. W. P.—The office of Worthy Matron is one of much labor, care, and anxiety, and demands the utmost attention and forbearance on the part of that officer.

The members will naturally look to you, not only for counsel in the many and varied matters that come before the Chapter, but for advice and sympathy in their troubles and sorrows. It should be your constant study, therefore, how best to cultivate all the social virtues.

You should be cautious in your behavior and courteous to your members. You should be an example of good order and punctuality, for in that manner only can you expect obedience to them from others. Within the Chapter it will be your duty to see that its regular meetings are held; that called meetings be had whenever the good of the Chapter demands it; that each of your subordinates fills her station with honor and usefulness; that the rules, by-laws and regulations be implicitly observed; that the funds, records, rituals and paraphernalia of the Chapter be properly preserved by the officers in whose charge they are; that the cry of the widow and orphan shall never be heard in vain within the sphere of operations assumed by this Chapter, and that it fails in nothing for which it is established.

The Matron of a Chapter should possess *knowledge,* to diversify her instructions; *judgment,* to preserve the happy medium between rashness and timidity; *talent,* to address the members at length on every emergency; *tact,* to conciliate disputes and reconcile contending parties; and *presence of mind,* to decide correctly on any sudden indiscretion or irregularity which may occur among the members of the Chapter, that order and good feeling may be perfect and complete. The great secret of government is to understand correctly under what circumstances authority should be exercised, and when it should be profitably withheld. She must never exercise partiality, or be detected in the slightest bias in favor of individuals. The Sister who possess *all these qualifications* will rule and govern her Chapter with honor to herself and satisfaction to the members; it will represent a well-regulated and happy family where harmony and loving kindness will prevail throughout the Chapter.

All this lies in your power to do, by the zealous

exercise of your prerogatives as Worthy Matron, to which office your associate members have been pleased to elect you.

Sister Marshal, you will now invest our Sister with the proper badge of her office.

When she has done so, the Patron continues:

Your badge, the Gavel within the Star, the highest emblem of authority, will admonish you, that upon your judgment and discretion rests the government of this Chapter and, in a great measure, the prosperity of our beautiful Order in this place.

Sister Marshal, you will now conduct our Sister to her proper station in the East.

The Marshal conducts her to the East, at the right of the Installing Officer, when the following, or some other ode, may be sung:

Music—*Zorah.*

Accept the trust we offer thee,
  Our Matron and our guide;
May justice, truth, and purpose high,
  In all thy power abide.

Oh! lead us by the light of truth,
  To walk in wisdom's way,
Through all the trying paths of life,
  To realms of endless day.

The Matron will be seated in the East until the other officers are installed.

ASSOCIATE MATRON

I. W. P.—Sister Marshal, you will now present the Associate Matron elect for installation.

I. MAR.—Worthy Patron, it affords me pleasure to present to you Sister ...., who has been elected Associate Matron of this Chapter for the ensuing year.

I. W. P.—My Sister, the duties of your position are embodied in the name of your office. You are the Assistant to the Worthy Matron in all branches of her responsible charge, and in her absence will succeed to all her privileges and responsibilities. It is necessary, therefore, that you should make yourself familiar with the duties of that office, so that you may fill it with credit to yourself and honor to your Chapter. Will you sacredly promise to use your utmost endeavors to make yourself useful and your station honorable in the post of Associate Matron?

ANS.—I do.

Sister Marshal, you will invest our Sister with the proper badge of her office.

She does so, and the Patron continues:

Your badge, the Sun within the Star, an emblem of brightness, admonishes you to assist the Worthy Matron by your counsel, as the rising sun enlightens the day, being ever ready to assume her station when should she be absent.

Sister Marshal, you will now conduct our Sister to her proper station in the West.

TREASURER

I. W. P.—Sister Marshal, you will now present the Treasurer elect.

I. MAR.—Worthy Patron, I take pleasure in presenting to you Sister ...., Treasurer-elect of this Chapter for the ensuing year.

I. W. P.—My Sister, the proper preservation of our funds demands the utmost honesty and care upon the part of the Treasurer. The money placed in your hands may be required for the relief of the widow and orphan whom God may, at the most unexpected moments, send us as objects of our bounty. Will you sacredly promise never to violate the sacred obligations assumed by you as Treasurer of this Chapter?

ANS.—I do.

Then, Sister Marshal, you will invest our Sister with the proper badge of her office.

She does so, and the Patron continues:

Your badge, the Crossed Keys within the Star, an emblem of security, admonishes you to the strictest fidelity in the preservation and disbursement of the funds entrusted to your keeping.

Sister Marshall, you will now conduct our Sister to her proper station in the Northeast.

SECRETARY

I. W. P.—Sister Marshal, you will now present the Secretary-elect.

I. MAR.—Worthy Patron, I have the pleasure of presenting to you Sister ...., who has been elected Secretary of this Chapter for the ensuing year.

I. W. P.—My Sister, yours is an onerous and most responsible charge. But few are competent to perform it in the thorough manner it demands. Failure or neglect upon your part will complicate and embarrass all our proceedings, and give us a disgraceful record on the books of the Grand Chapter. It is your duty to note down in proper order the business of our meetings; to collect all monies due the Chapter, and to make out and forward to the Grand Secretary the necessary returns as required by the Constitution. With this knowledge of the responsible labors which, as Secretary, will be expected of you, do you sacredly promise to perform them to the utmost of your ability?

ANS.—I do.

Then, Sister Marshal, you will invest our Sister with the proper badge of her office.

She does so, and the Patron continues:

Your badge, the Crossed Pens within the Star, an emblem of power and intelligence, admonishes you that, as an invisible pen records all our thoughts and actions, so should you record the good deeds of your companions, and keep the accounts between them and the Chapter without prejudice or partiality.

Sister Marshal, you will now conduct our Sister to her proper station in the Southeast.

CONDUCTRESSES

I. W. P.—Sister Marshal, you will now present the Conductress and Associate Conductress-elect.

I. MAR.—Worthy Patron, it is my pleasing duty to introduce Sister ...., elected to be Conductress, and Sister ...., elected to be Associate Conductress, of this Chapter for the ensuing year.

I. W. P.—My Sisters, upon you devolve the duty of preparing and conducting through the ceremonies those who seek the privileges of our Order; it is necessary, therefore, that you should be among our most enlightened officers. The candidate enters our Chapter with a heart open to receive a favorable impression of our mysteries and our aims. If you present these matters aright, throwing sisterly courtesy and dignity around your official proceedings, she will acquire a fond regard for a system that aims so high and promises so much. Remember, therefore, that it depends greatly upon the manner in which you receive and conduct a candidate to make those impressions lasting, and what we desire they should be.

Such, my Sisters, are your duties as Conductress and Associate Conductress, and do you now pledge yourselves to use your best endeavors to perform them with credit to yourselves and honor to the Chapter?

ANS.—I do.

Then, Sister Marshal, you will invest our Sisters with their respective badges of office.

She does so, and the Patron continues:

Sister Conductress, your badge, the Scroll and Baton within the Star, an emblem of prepared plans and their fulfilment, admonishes you that the first impressions made upon a candidate are permanent, and should always be for good.

Sister Associate Conductress, your badge, the Baton within the Star, an emblem of direction, admonishes you that good discipline is essential to the success of our society.

Sister Marshal and Brother Marshal, you will now conduct our Sisters to their proper stations in the South and North.

TRUSTEE

I. W. P.—Sister Marshal, you will now present the Trustee-elect for .... years.

I. MAR.—Worthy Patron, I present Sister ...., elected to serve .... years as Trustee of this Chapter.

I. W. P.—My Sister, the Trustees are the custodians of the property, regalia, investments and securities of the Chapter and are subject to the direction of the Chapter in all matters. Yours is a position of trust and responsibility and the Chapter has elected you with the expectation and belief that you will exercise as great care over its property and funds as you would over your own.

Sister Marshal, you will invest our Sister with the proper badge of her office.

She does so and Patron continues:

Your badge, a Key within the Star, admonishes you to guard and protect the interests of the Chapter.

Sister Marshal, you will now conduct our Sister to her proper place in the room.

(NOTE: *Material set in italics is for* OPTIONAL *officers.*)

FLAG BEARERS

I. W. P.—Sister Marshal, you will now present the Flag Bearer(s).

I. MAR.—Worthy Patron, I take pleasure in presenting Sister ...., who has been appointed

INSTALLATION OF OFFICERS 199

Christian Flag Bearer, Sister ...., appointed National Flag Bearer, and Sister ...., appointed Eastern Star Flag Bearer, for the ensuing year.

I. W. P.—Sister ...., it is your duty to carry the Christian Flag and place it in the East. It is the only flag which takes precedence over all others.

Sister ...., it is your duty to carry the Flag of the United States of America and to place it in its honored position in the East.

Sister ...., it is your duty to carry the Eastern Star Flag and to place it in the East.

Sister Marshal, you will invest our Sisters with their respective badges of office.

She does so and Patron continues:

Sister Christian Flag Bearer, your badge, the Christian Flag within the Star, an emblem of the banner of the Prince of Peace, stands for no one creed or denomination and should remind you of the blessings and privileges which we enjoy in this country that has known the light of Christianity.

Sister National Flag Bearer, your badge, the United States Flag within the Star, an emblem of liberty and justice for all, admonishes you that patriotism is essential in good citizenship.

Sister Eastern Star Flag Bearer, your badge, the Eastern Star Flag within the Star, is symbolic of the characters of the 5 Heroines and admonishes you to practice the lessons of these Heroines in your daily life. Sis. Mar. and Bro. Mar., you will conduct our Sisters to their proper stations.

CHAPLAIN

I. W. P.—*Sis. Mar., you will present the Chaplain.*

I. MAR.—*W. P., I present Sis. . . . . who has been appointed Chaplain for the ensuing year.*

I. W. P.—*My Sister, it is your duty to lead the Chapter in its devotions at the altar and to invoke the blessings of our Heavenly Father on our work. Sis. Mar., invest our Sister with the badge of her office.— Your badge, the Open Bible within the Star, is an emblem of the Word of God, admonishing you to walk uprightly that your life may be void of offense toward God and man. Sis. Mar., escort the Chaplain to her station.*

MARSHAL

I. W. P.—Sis. Mar., you will now present the Mar.

I. MAR.—W. P., I present Sis. . . . ., who has been appointed Marshal of this Chap. for the ensuing year.

I. W. P.—My Sister, it is your duty to escort the flags to their positions in the East, to respond to the roll call of officers, and to conduct the processions of the Chapter. Sis. Mar., invest our Sister with the proper badge of her office.—Your badge, the Crossed Batons within the Star, a symbol of order and discipline, admonishes you that diligence is essential in the performance of duty. Sis. Mar., you will conduct our Sister to her proper station.

MUSICIAN

I. W. P.—Sister Marshal, you will now present the Musician.

I. MAR.—Worthy Patron, I present Sister . . . . , who has been appointed Musician of this Chapter for the ensuing year.

I. W. P.—My Sister, it is your duty to furnish the music for the ceremonies and enjoyment of the Chapter.

Sister Marshal, you will invest our Sister with the proper badge of her office.

> She does so and Patron continues:

Your badge, the Lyre within the Star, an emblem of music and poetry, admonishes you that harmony is essential in the work of our Order.

Sister Marshal, you will now conduct our Sister to her proper station.

WARDER AND SENTINEL

I. W. P.—Sister Marshal, you will now present the Warder and the Sentinel of the Chapter.

I. MAR.—Worthy Patron, I present to you for installation Sister . . . . , appointed as Warder, and Brother[1] . . . . , appointed as Sentinel of this Chapter for the ensuing year.

I. W. P.—My Sister and Brother, you are respec-

---
[1] *If both are Sisters, the language must be changed accordingly.*

tively the Inner and Outer Guards of this Chapter. Upon you, therefore, we rely to preserve that secrecy which is essential to our proceedings, and to see that the solemnity of our ceremonies is not interrupted by untimely alarm.

Will you solemnly promise to use your utmost endeavors to promote that state of harmony and serenity which becomes all our proceedings?

ANS.—I do.

Then, Sister Marshal, you will invest our Sister and Brother with their respective badges of office.

She does so, and Patron continues:

Sister Warder, your badge, the Dove within the Star, an emblem of peace, admonishes you that peace and harmony are essentially necessary to the success of our Order, and that it lies greatly in your power to promote them.

Brother Sentinel, your badge, the Crossed Swords within the Star, an emblem of protection, admonishes you that upon your watchful care depends our security against interruption.

Sister Marshal and Brother Marshal, you will now conduct our Sister and Brother to their proper stations.

STAR POINTS

I. W. P.—Sister Marshal, you will now present the Sisters appointed to represent the five rays of the Central Star of this Chapter.

INSTALLATION OF OFFICERS

I. MAR.—Worthy Patron, it is my pleasing duty to present in one group the five rays of this Chapter of the Eastern Star: Sister ...... has been appointed to represent the blue ray of Adah; Sister ......, the yellow ray of Ruth; Sister ......, the white ray of Esther; Sister ......, the green ray of Martha; and Sister ...., the red ray of Electa.

I. W. P.—My Sisters, you are the floral center of this Chapter, and as the various flowers which your colors represent, illuminated by that great light, the Holy Scriptures, teach us the lessons of undying love, unending possession, heart purity, undeviating sincerity, and unfading beauty, so are represented in you the most charming, the most pathetic, and the most instructive lessons of the Old and New Testament.

To you is assigned the duty of instructing the candidate in those sublime virtues, illustrated in the lives of the characters you represent. How important then, that in your official duties you should labor to throw an air of beauty and solemnity around all that you have to say and do, so that from you, as the Central Star of our Chapter, may emanate a light that will give holy joy to every one who attends our meeting.

Will you promise to use your utmost endeavors to fulfill those duties with dignity and earnestness?

ANS.—I do.

Sister Marshal, you will invest our Sisters with their respective badges of office.

The Marshal invests them with their jewels, beginning with Adah. The Patron continues:

I. W. P.—Sister Adah, your badge, the Sword and Veil, will remind you of the filial piety of the heroic daughter of Jephthah.

Sister Ruth, your badge, the Sheaf, will remind you that to please God is worthy of our greatest sacrifices.

Sister Esther, your badge, the Crown and Scepter, will remind you that true friendship refuses no pain or loss for the object of its affection.

Sister Martha, your badge, the Broken Column, will remind you that times of the deepest sorrow and loneliness are often enlightened by the highest graces of God.

Sister Electa, your badge, the Cup, will remind you that the cup which our Heavenly Father gives us to drink, though bitter and distasteful, will in the end prove to overflow with blessings, rich, abounding and eternal. Such, my Sisters, are the lessons inculcated by your several badges of office.

The truly sublime virtues exemplified in the lives of those you represent are worthy of imitation, and I hope that as you teach these virtues in the Chapter, so will you practice them out of it. Thus will you not only honor the stations to which you

INSTALLATION OF OFFICERS

have been appointed, but lay up for yourselves those Heavenly treasures that shall never fade, and will render you "Fairest among thousands altogether lovely."

Sister Marshal and Brother Marshal, you will now conduct these Sisters to their proper stations.

ASSOCIATE PATRON

I. W. P.—Sister Marshal, you will now present the Associate Patron-elect.

I. MAR.—Worthy Patron, I take pleasure in presenting to you Brother ...., who has been elected Associate Patron of this Chapter for the ensuing year.

I. W. P.—My Brother, your duties are to assist the Worthy Patron and, in case of his absence, to assume his station and to perform his duties. It will be your duty to study the laws, rules and regulations of the Order and to make yourself proficient in the ritualistic work of the Order of the Eastern Star that you may be prepared to exercise the higher position to which you may be called at any moment.

Sister Marshal, you will invest our Brother with the proper badge of his office.

She does so, and Patron continues:

Your badge, the Rayed Star within the Star, is an emblem of Divine Guidance and admonishes you to be faithful to your fraternal obligation.

Sister Marshal, you will now conduct our Brother to his proper station in the West.

WORTHY PATRON

I. W. P.—Sister Marshal, you will now present the Worthy Patron-elect.

I. MAR.—Worthy Patron, I have the honor to present for installation Bro. ....., elected Worthy Patron of this Chapter for the ensuing year. Our brother is fully aware of the great responsibilities he is assuming in the acceptance of this important position, yet he is willing to undertake the charge in the belief that, with the aid and forbearance of the members and brethren, he will not fail in the performance of his duty, and thus prove that the confidence reposed in him has not been misplaced.

I. W. P.—Bro. ....., you have been elected by the free choice of the members of this Chapter to occupy the most exalted position in their power to bestow upon a gentleman, a just compliment to your zeal and worth, and for which I offer you my sincere congratulations. Your long and intimate acquaintance with the rules and affairs of our Order justify me in saying that your fellow members have

INSTALLATION OF OFFICERS

exercised a sound discretion in this selection. You are elevated to a position from which the power and prerogative may depart with the expiration of your term of service, but the honor and dignity, except by your own act, *never*.

The high honors attached to the office of Worthy Patron are accompanied by weighty and delicate responsibilities. From the nature of this association, you are not the chief officer, yet, in all things pertaining to your station, your advice and counsel will always be solicited, and your decisions cheerfully approved. It is your duty to see that the ritualistic work is properly exemplified. It is expected that you will not only have a watchful care over the interests of the Chapter, and see that the laws of the Order are promptly obeyed by the members, but that you will feel called upon to exemplify in your conduct through life the excellent tenets of our Order. Prove, by your good example, that the members of the Chapter have found in you a brother in whom they can perfectly confide. Maintain with unswerving care the constitutions and regulations of the Order, and, in your respect for law and good government, cause all others to find the strongest incentive of obedience to all lawful commands.

Sister Marshal, you will invest our Brother with the proper badge of his office.

She does so, and Patron continues:

Your badge, the Square and Compasses within the Star, is an emblem of the relationship existing between the Masonic fraternity and the Order of the Eastern Star, and admonishes you to be ever mindful of your obligations to both.

Sister Marshal, you will now conduct our Brother to his proper station in the East, at the left of the Worthy Matron.

I. W. P.—Worthy Matron, the officers of your Chapter have been installed into their respective stations for the ensuing year. You will now receive in charge the Charter, by the authority of which this Chapter is held. You will carefully preserve it, and in no case should it ever be out of your immediate control; and when your term of office expires, you will duly transmit it to your successor in office.

You will receive the Constitution of the Grand Chapter of the State, and the By-laws of this Chapter, which you are to see are carefully and promptly obeyed.

The Bible—that book which reveals the duties which the Great Master of all exacts from us, has God for its author, truth for its substance, and the salvation of mankind for its end—open upon the altar, is confided to your care.

And now I present you with this Gavel, emblem of your authority; and as no one can disobey it, I confidently hope that you will never use it in an arbitrary or dictatorial manner, remembering that we should charitably temper justice with equity.

The Chapter is now called up, *** and Patron continues:

Worthy Matron and Worthy Patron, behold your Sisters and Brothers.

Sisters and Brothers, behold your Worthy Matron and Worthy Patron, and as such you will salute them with the honors.

The honors are given.
The Chapter is called down * by the Installing Patron.

I. W. P.—Sisters and Brothers, of ...... Chapter, No. .., such is the nature of all associations, that, as some must rule and govern, so others must submit and obey.

The officers whom you have selected to preside over your deliberations during the ensuing year, are, I believe, sufficiently conversant with the rules of propriety to avoid exceeding the powers with which you have intrusted them.

A leading object of our institution is to inculcate sound morality, as founded upon the great moral principle set forth in the sacred volume, ever found upon our Altar, which we receive as the rule and guide of our faith and practice. Special care should be used in the admission of members, lest, by the introduction of improper materials, the institution would be injured. It should be constantly borne in mind that the respectability and usefulness of a Chapter does not consist in the number, but in the character of its members. It is better that no additions be made to the roll of membership, than even one unworthy foot should be allowed to cross the threshold of the Chapter. The uninitiated judge of our institution by the conduct of its individual members. You should be as careful of the reputation of your Chapter as of that of your family.

All things are now ready for you to enter upon the proceedings of a new year. But we know not what is before us. No one can affirm that another year, or even a single day, will be committed to our trust. Therefore, if we have been faithful heretofore, let us redouble our exertions for the future.

Let us be kind, forbearing, and forgiving, one toward another. Let us sacredly preserve our lips from slander and evil speaking. And, finally, let us ever be governed, in words and deeds, by that golden rule, "That whatsoever ye would that others should do unto you, do ye even so unto them." Thus may we confidently hope that in the good providence of God, each of us will be brought, through a useful and happy life, to a blissful close, and a triumphant entrance into the city of the living God.

Sister Marshal, you will now proclaim the officers

INSTALLATION OF OFFICERS 211

of ...... Chapter No. .. regularly elected, appointed, and installed.

The Installing Mar. is escorted to the East by the Assistant Mar. She ascends the dais in the East and is handed the gavel by the Installing Patron. Installing Marshal calls up the Chapter with ***.

I. MAR.—In the name of the Grand Chapter of the Order of the Eastern Star of the State of ...., and by direction of Brother ...., Installing Patron, I proclaim the Officers of ...... Chapter No. .. regularly elected,[1] appointed, and installed for the ensuing year. * (*Gives one blow with the gavel and hands it back to the Installing Patron.*)

I. Mar. then leaves the East and is escorted to her former position West of the Altar by the Assistant Mar. who has been standing at the foot of the dais.

The I. W. P. thanks them for their services and the Installing Marshals take their seats.

I. W. P.—You will now assume your station as Worthy Matron. *

He hands the gavel to the newly installed Matron who thanks him for his services and she continues with the meeting.

MUSIC

---

[1] *Any officer not elected, appointed, or installed, must be referred to as an exception.*

INSTALLATION OF THE OFFICERS OF A GRAND CHAPTER

The Grand Patron of the preceding year, or a Past Grand Patron, should preside at the Installation of Grand Chapter Officers.

An officer of a Masonic Grand Lodge, or the Master of a Lodge, may perform this service, assisted by a Grand Marshal.

The chairs remain occupied by the officers who, having served their time, are about to retire from office.

INST. OFFICER—Sisters and Brothers, I am now prepared to install into their respective stations the officers of this Grand Chapter. Brother Grand Marshal, you will present the officers-elect at the Altar for installation.

The officers are arranged by the Grand Marshal in a semicircle around the Altar, facing the East, the Grand Patron on the right, the Grand Matron next, and so on according to rank.

GR. MAR.—Grand Patron, the Grand Officers-elect are in order before you, and await your pleasure.

INST. OFF.—Sisters and Brothers, you here behold those whom you have elected officers to serve you for the ensuing year. If any member of this Grand Chapter is apprised of any just or sufficient reason why any of these officers should

INSTALLATION OF GRAND OFFICERS

not be installed, let the objection be now made known.

No objection being made, he proceeds:

I will now administer the obligation of office, which you will each repeat.

The Grand Chapter is called up by three raps of the gavel. * * *

I (*each giving full name*) do solemnly pledge my honor, in the presence of Almighty God and of this Grand Chapter of the Order of the Eastern Star, that I will, to the best of my ability, faithfully and impartially, perform all the duties incumbent on the office to which I have been selected; that I will conform to the constitution, laws, rules and regulations of this Grand Chapter, and in every way within my power assist in extending the usefulness of the Institution.

The officers may be seated on one side of the room convenient to be presented in succession. The Grand Chapter is called to order. *

GRAND PATRON

Brother Grand Marshal, you will present the Grand Patron for installation.

GR. MAR.—Worthy Sir, I have the honor to present Brother ...., who has been elected Grand Patron of the Grand Chapter, Order of the

Eastern Star, of the State of ......, for the ensuing year.

INST. OFF.—My Brother, we most cordially congratulate you upon your election to this, the most distinguished and important office within the gift of your associates. The confidence displayed by this Grand Chapter in elevating you to supreme command is an ample guarantee to the Order throughout this jurisdiction of your wisdom and of your worth. You cannot, Sir, be otherwise than aware of the deep and solemn consequence of the duties you are now about to assume, or of the many cares and perplexities which surround its exalted honors. These difficulties will, I am confident, be alleviated by the affectionate sympathy and active assistance of your associates. You may occasionally encounter stern opposition from without, from those who do not, or will not understand our purposes; but as the most dangerous and insidious enemy to the perpetuity and harmony of our beloved institution will pale before you in the uprightness of your administration of its affairs, we can have no fears of the results.

We now, Sir, have the honor to invest you with the jewel of your office (*the Marshal invests him with the jewel*), and with the emblem of your control (*hands the gavel*), which in your hands should never be sounded in vain, and welcome you to the East of the Grand Chapter, Order of the Eastern

Star, of the State of ...., and render you this, the first act of homage due to you as Grand Patron.

Bows low, with hands crossed on the breast. The Grand Chapter is called up. ***

I now salute and proclaim you Grand Patron of the Order of the Eastern Star, of the State of .... Sisters and Brothers, behold your Grand Patron. Grand Patron, behold your Sisters and Brothers.

The assembly will, under the direction of the Installing Officer, salute the Grand Patron with the grand honors. *

GRAND MATRON

Grand Marshal, you will present the Grand Matron-elect for installation.

GR. MAR.—I have the honor to present to you Sister ...., who has been elected Grand Matron of this Grand Chapter for the ensuing year.

INST. OFF.—Sister ......, the office to which you have been elected is one of high dignity, and may become one of great importance, for in the absence of the Grand Patron from the meetings of the Grand Chapter, or from the limits of its jurisdiction, you are, by the Constitution, invested with his powers and to exercise his high prerogatives. In view of such emergencies, allow us to remind you of the duty devolving on you, to be thoroughly prepared to fill his distinguished position with honor to yourself and advantage to the Order.

With pleasure we invest you with the jewel of office, and proclaim you Grand Matron of the Order of the Eastern Star of the State of ......
*** Sisters and Brothers, behold your Grand Matron. Grand Matron, behold your Sisters and Brothers.

Sisters and Brothers, you will with me, salute the Grand Matron with the grand honors. (*done*) *

You will be seated in your place, at the right of the Grand Patron.

The Grand Marshal will present the following officers, as requested by the Installing Officer, in the same manner as the previous officers.

ASSOCIATE GRAND PATRON

INST. OFF.—Brother ......, by the suffrages of the members of this Grand Chapter, you have been elected to the position of Associate Grand Patron. Be assiduous in the performance of your duties, so that you will truly be a strength and support to the Grand Patron. In the absence of your superior officers, you will assume supreme command. Your fitness for the discharge of such a trust undoubtedly led to your selection for the office by your companions, and it will be your duty and, no doubt, a pleasure so to act as to justify their confidence.

You will now be invested with the jewel of your office and conducted to your station in the West.

ASSOCIATE GRAND MATRON

INST. OFF.—Sister ...., your associates have shown their confidence in your fidelity by electing you to the responsible position of Associate Grand Matron. Your previous devotion to the duties of the Order of the Eastern Star is a sufficient guarantee that you will be a vigilant officer in whatever station you may be placed. It affords us much pleasure to have you invested with the jewel of your office.

You will be conducted to your station, in the West, at the right of the Associate Grand Patron.

GRAND TREASURER

INST. OFF.—Sister ......, your associates have been pleased to elect you to the responsible office of Treasurer of this Grand Chapter. Your integrity and truthfulness satisfy us that the trust is wisely reposed. It is your duty to receive all monies from the Grand Secretary; make due entry of the same, and pay them out on the order of the Grand Chapter, or Grand Patron, rendering accounts thereof. We are happy to have the privilege of investing you with the jewel of your office. The faithful performance of your duties will entitle you to the good opinion and thanks of your companions. You will be conducted to your station.

GRAND SECRETARY

INST. OFF.—Brother[1] ......, it is with extreme pleasure that we invest you with the jewel of your office. The duties of Grand Secretary are more varied, difficult, and I may add, pleasant, than those of any other officer in the Grand Chapter. Brought by your official position more immediately into communication with the whole body of the Order, it is requisite that you should possess ability, skill and industry, to meet the various demands upon you. It is your duty to record all the proceedings of the Grand Chapter; to receive all monies due the Grand Chapter, and pay them over to the Grand Treasurer, and keep a just and true account of the same; to keep and affix the seal of the Grand Chapter to all proper documents, and carefully to preserve its archives. These are very important duties, on which, in a great measure, the usefulness of the Grand Chapter depends. Accuracy and punctuality are qualities which your office particularly requires; and as there is no place in the Grand Chapter in which a member can render more substantial service to the Order, I am

---

[1] *When this office is held by a lady the language must be changed.*

confident that you will so perform its duties as to merit their esteem and receive their hearty approbation. You will be conducted to your station.

GRAND CONDUCTRESS

INST. OFF.—Sister ......, you have been elected to the honorable post of Grand Conductress of this Grand Chapter, and will now be invested with the jewel of office. Upon you will devolve the duties of receiving and introducing visitors; acting as the messenger of the Grand Officers; and as a useful assistant to the Grand Marshal in the ceremonies of the Order. Thus your official position becomes one of great value and importance to the comfort and good order of the Grand Chapter. Vigilance and zeal are necessary requisites of your office, and we are confident that you possess these qualifications. You will be conducted to your station, in the South.

ASSOCIATE GRAND CONDUCTRESS

INST. OFF.—Sister ......, you have been elected Associate Grand Conductress, and will now be invested with the jewel of office. Your duties will require you to devote your attention to the condition of the Grand Chapter; to see that everything is in readiness for the meetings of the body; to act as special messenger of the Grand Patron and Grand Matron, and to assist the Grand Marshal and Grand Conductress in the performance of their duties. You will now be conducted to your station in the North; and remember that the post of honor is the post of duty.

GRAND CHAPLAIN

INST. OFF.—Reverend and Worthy Brother, the sacred position of Grand Chaplain has been entrusted to your care. In the discharge of your duties you will be required to lead the devotional exercises of the sessions of the Grand Chapter, and to perform the sacred functions of your holy calling at all our public ceremonies. The principles and precepts of our association are in strict accordance with the best teachings and maxims found in the inspired volume, which is the chart and text-book of your sacred mission. Teach us from its life-giving precepts; intercede for us with that Divine Majesty which it so fully reveals and unfolds to us; and inspire us by its lessons of infinite wisdom and truth. The profession which you have chosen for your lot in life is the best guarantee that you will discharge the duties of your present appointment with steadfastness and perseverance in well-doing. It is eminently appropriate that an emblem of the sacred volume, which sheds its benignant rays upon the altar of every lawful assemblage of our Order, should be the jewel of your office, with which you will now be invested and

GRAND TRUSTEES, FLAG BEARERS AND MUSICIAN

If these officers are in the Grand Chapter, they should also be installed and the presenting of them should be similar to the other Grand Officers. See Installation of Officers for Subordinate Chapters for their respective duties.

GRAND MARSHAL

INST. OFF.—Brother ......, you have been appointed Grand Marshal of this Grand Chapter. The duties of your office require care, promptness, and activity. You are to arrange all processions of the Grand Chapter; to make the proclamations of the installations of the Grand Officers, and at the institution of new Chapters, under direction of the Grand Patron. Skill and precision are essentially necessary to the faithful discharge of these duties. You will now be invested with the jewel of your office, and be conducted to your station, at the left, in front of the Grand Patron.

GRAND LECTURER

INST. OFF.—Brother ......, you have been appointed Grand Lecturer and the Custodian of the Ritual of the Order in this jurisdiction, and we now invest you with the jewel of your office. It is your duty to instruct the members of the Order in the proper performance of their duties; to communicate light and information to the uninformed; to preserve our Ritual from change and innovation; and, by your instructions to the members, to illustrate the genius and vindicate the principles of our institution. Let it be your object, while inculcating upon the members of this Order a faithful regard for its obligations, to impress upon them a favorable opinion of its moral design and intellectual tendency. You will be conducted to your station at the left, in front of the Grand Patron.

GRAND WARDER

INST. OFF.—Sister ......, you have been elected Grand Warder of this Grand Chapter, and we now invest you with the jewel of your office. Your position is one of trust and responsibility. It is your duty to announce the approach of visitors and strangers. In so doing, possess yourself of the necessary information to announce their rank and position properly. Be cautious and vigilant, that no improper person may gain admittance. Your station is inside, at the door of entrance, on the right of the Associate Grand Matron.

GRAND ADAH, GRAND RUTH, GRAND ESTHER, GRAND MARTHA, AND GRAND ELECTA

INST. OFF.—Sisters, you have been appointed severally to the offices of Grand Adah, Grand

Ruth, Grand Esther, Grand Martha, and Grand Electa. You are required to assist the Grand Officers generally in the discharge of their duties, and in every way in your power aid in the promotion of the interests of the Grand Chapter and the success of the Order. During the opening ceremonies of the Grand Chapter you will proclaim those sublime lessons of purity and faithfulness as exemplified by the same characters in the subordinate Chapter. You will be invested with the jewels of your several offices, and conducted to your stations.

GRAND SENTINEL

INST. OFF.—Brother ......, you have been appointed Grand Sentinel of the Grand Chapter. Our institution is of a sacred character, and an irreparable injury might result from a negligent or careless discharge of your duty. Your office is one of great importance, and requires unremitting care and watchfulness. Your station is outside the door. We now invest you with the jewel of your office, and you will repair to your place, and there be in active discharge of your duties.

All the officers are called up. **

INST. OFF.—It has fallen to your lot to be elevated to the highest places in the gift of this Grand Chapter. On entering upon the responsible duties of your several offices the members of this Grand Body expect you to devote yourselves with energy and zeal to the work allotted you to do. I need not remind you of the solemn obligations you have entered into with us, and that on you will depend much of our prosperity, harmony and success. May you be guided in the discharge of your duties by the spirit of the principles set forth in the sublime teachings of our Order. May the self-sacrificing spirit of Adah, the meekness of Ruth, the devotion of Esther, the faith of Martha, and the love of Electa, be examples for your imitation, being assured that the more devoted you are to our principles, the greater will be the respect entertained for you by the members of the Order, and the greater will be your enjoyment while you remain with us.

In the organization of our Society, it is necessary that some should rule and others serve. A wise ruler seeks to elevate those to whom he is indebted for the position he occupies, and as a stream cannot rise higher than its source, so a ruler cannot gain prominence and glory greater than that enjoyed by his subjects. Let it be your aim to dignify your office, for, in so doing, you elevate the Grand Chapter, and bring glory and honor to our beloved Order.

Everyone is called up. ***

Sisters and Brothers, let us all remember that we have a personal interest as well as a personal duty in the welfare of our Order and that in proportion to our energy and zeal will be our success and prosperity. Let us feel assured that in all branches of our Order the progress, zeal and good conduct of the *members* are modeled upon the fidelity of the *officers,* and so be animated by the highest sense of duty. Let me exhort you in the words of the great Apostle: Do all things without murmurings and without disputings; that you may be without blame, without spot, the children of God, irreproachable, in the midst of a people depraved and perverse, amongst whom you shine as lights in the world, bearing to them the word of life; so that in the day of judgment we may all feel that we have not traveled in vain or vainly labored in the work of the Order of the Eastern Star.

Bro. Grand Marshal, you will proclaim the officers of the Grand Chapter elected appointed and installed.

The Grand Marshal will then go to the East and, standing upon the dais, will make the proclamation:

G. MAR.—By order of the Grand Patron and by authority of the Grand Chapter, Order of the Eastern Star, of the State of ...., I proclaim its Grand Officers, elected and appointed, and duly installed, in ample form. *

PARLIAMENTARY LAW ADAPTED TO A CHAPTER

The following Legislative Rules are appropriate for the government of a Chapter, for business:

1. The constitutional quorum (seven members and the charter) being present, the W. Matron, assisted by the other officers, opens the Chapter.

2. Calling the roll of officers, and reading the minutes of last meeting, for information.

3. The minutes of the current meeting must be read and approved before closing the Chapter.

4. Minutes of a special meeting may be read, but must be approved at a regular meeting.

5. A motion must be seconded and put to the Chapter before it can be considered.

6. A question containing several parts may be divided, upon the call of a member.

7. When a blank is to be filled, the question must be first taken on the longest time and the highest sum.

8. An amendment takes the place of the question it is proposed to amend, and must be decided first. An amendment to an amendment must be decided before the first amendment. A third

amendment to the original question is out of order.

9. When a motion is under debate, no motion shall be received but to lay on the table, to postpone indefinitely, to postpone to a certain day, to commit, or to amend; which several motions shall have precedence in the order here stated.

10. A motion to lay on the table is not debatable.

11. A motion to adjourn cannot be entertained.

12. A motion for the previous question cannot be entertained.

13. A motion to reconsider must be made by a member who voted with the majority.

14. Committees of the whole are not known in this Order.

15. All committees must be appointed by the chair unless otherwise specially provided for.

16. A majority of a committee must concur in a report; but a minority may also make a report.

17. Reports may be recommitted at any time before final action has been taken.

PETITION TO ORGANIZE A SUBORDINATE CHAPTER

To organize a Subordinate Chapter, seven ladies possessing harmony of sentiment and purpose, having received in a legal manner all the degrees of the Order, may petition the Grand Chapter in the following form.

To the M. E. Grand Patron of the .... Grand Chapter of the Adoptive Rite of the Order of the Eastern Star, Jurisdiction of ....

The undersigned, the wives, mothers, widows, sisters and daughters (*as the case may be*) of Master Masons, in good standing, and in possession of the five degrees of the Eastern Star, of the Adoptive Rite, as appears by the certificate annexed, being desirous of associating ourselves into a Subordinate Chapter of the Adoptive Rite, for the purposes of mutual aid, sympathy and relief, as contemplated in the Constitution and By-laws of the .... Grand Chapter, and for the greater extension of the Rite, do hereby solicit a Charter under the title of ...... Chapter, No. ...., to be holden at ...... County of ......, State of ......

We have selected and do recommend Sister ...... to be Worthy Matron, and Sister ..... to be Associate Matron, and would recommend the appointment of Brother ...... to be the Worthy Patron of said Chapter.

If the prayer of this petition shall be granted, we solemnly pledge ourselves to strictly conform to the constitutional requirements of the Grand Chapter in all things appertaining to the Adoptive Rite, and the edicts of the M. E. Grand Patron, when said edicts are not inconsistent with the Landmarks of the Rite; and if the Chapter herein solicited fail to become organized, or at any time hereafter be dissolved, we pledge our honor, each for herself and her successors, that the charter, books of record and account, and rituals shall be immediately returned to your Grand Secretary.

In token whereof, we have severally affixed our hands this .... day of ...., A.D. 19..
(*Signed by all the petitioners*)

This petition must be endorsed by the Deputy Grand Patron of the State, or by the Master of the Lodge nearest the place where the Chapter is to be located, and should be in this or similar form:

This is to certify that the names attached to the within petition are in their own proper handwriting, and are known or avouched to me as the (*naming their relationship to members of the Masonic Order*), all of whom have received the degrees of the Eastern Star.

I, therefore, fraternally recommend granting the prayer of the petitioners.

(Signed)

....
Master of ..... Lodge, No. ...., at ...

CONSTITUTING AND INAUGURATING A CHAPTER

The following ceremonies may be used when a new Chapter of the Order of the Eastern Star is to be Constituted and Inaugurated and its officers installed by a Grand Patron, assisted by officers of the Grand Chapter. An authorized Deputy performing this service will make the necessary changes.

The Chapter room should be arranged as for work; and, if convenient, it may be decorated with flowers, and music introduced during the ceremonies.

If the Chapter has been previously working, it may be opened in the ordinary manner. If not, the officers-elect will take their seats in the room, and the assembly be called to order by the Worthy Matron-elect.

When a Grand Patron, or his representative, performs the ceremony, the officers of the Grand Chapter will assemble in an adjoining room, and form a procession in the following order:

CONSTITUTING AND INAUGURATING 231

FLAG BEARERS

GRAND MARSHAL	GRAND CONDUCTRESS
ASSOCIATE GRAND CONDUCTRESS	GRAND ADAH
	GRAND RUTH
GRAND ELECTA	GRAND ESTHER
GRAND MARTHA	GRAND WARDER
GRAND LECTURER	GRAND SECRETARY
GRAND TREASURER	GRAND TRUSTEE
GRAND TRUSTEE	GRAND MUSICIAN
GRAND TRUSTEE	
ASSOCIATE GRAND MATRON	ASSOCIATE GRAND PATRON
GRAND CHAPLAIN, carrying a Bible	
GRAND MATRON	GRAND PATRON

The G.P. (in the outer room) directs the G.C., accompanied by the G.Mar., to enter the Chapter room to inform the Matron-elect of his readiness to constitute and inaugurate the Chapter and to install its officers.

As the G.C. enters the room, the W.M.-elect will call up all in the room with * * *.

G. COND.—Worthy Matron-elect, I am directed by the Grand Patron of the Grand Chapter to inform you that he is now ready to constitute and inaugurate this Chapter and install its officers.

MATRON—Grand Conductress, please convey to the Grand Patron our thanks, and inform him that we are ready to obey any orders he may transmit to us.*

The Grand Conductress retires, and repeats to the Grand Patron the response of the Matron elect. The Grand Patron says:

G. P.—The Chapter duly convened is prepared to receive us. Let us proceed to perform the duty for which we have assembled.

MUSIC

The door is thrown open. The Matron gives with the gavel *** calling up all in the room, and the procession enters, passing to the right and left of the altar, bringing the Grand Patron and Grand Matron to the center. The Grand Patron and Grand Matron are invited to the East.

MATRON-ELECT—Worthy Brother ...., Grand Patron and Worthy Sister ...., Grand Matron, in behalf of the Sisters and Brothers here present, I bid you and the other Grand Officers a cordial welcome. Sisters Conductress and Associate Conductress you will escort the Grand Patron and Grand Matron to the East.

After they have ascended the dais the Matron-elect will introduce them to members present:

MATRON-ELECT—Sisters and Brothers, it is my great pleasure to present to you our Grand Patron and Grand Matron. You will join with me in saluting these distinguished Grand Officers with the grand honors.

After grand honors, the Matron-elect hands the gavel to Grand Patron and says:

MATRON-ELECT—Grand Patron, under any circumstances, your presence among us would be hailed with pleasure, as a fortunate event, but it is now especially acceptable, when you come bearing the glad tidings of your intention to constitute and inaugurate us permanently into a Chapter of the Order of the Eastern Star, with power to perform our part in the great work of charity, benevolence, and loving kindness. Be pleased, dear sir, to receive from us assurances that we are anxious to prove ourselves worthy of the privilege of laboring to promote the best interests of our beloved Order, and that we are willing to assume the duties and responsibilities which additional powers for good will impose upon us.

G. P.—Worthy Matron, we thank you and your associates for your cordial welcome and good wishes; and we cannot too much commend the sentiments you have expressed. We reciprocate your kind feelings, and fully concur in what you have so wisely said. If the body over which you preside shall continue to be actuated by those principles, it cannot fail to attain high honor and do good service to the noble cause you all have most generously espoused.

We shall now proceed to constitute and inaugurate your Chapter, and install its officers.

The officers of the new Chapter about to be constituted will vacate their stations and the officers of the Grand Chapter will assume them. *

The Grand Marshal will seat the officers of the new Chapter together on one side of the room, in order. The jewels will be collected and placed in readiness for installation. A suitable Ode may be sung. When the singing is concluded, the Grand Patron says:

G. P.—At the recent session, and upon due deliberation, the Grand Chapter granted to the members of this Chapter a Charter, establishing and confirming them in the rights and privileges of a regularly constituted Chapter of the Order of the Eastern Star, which the Grand Secretary will now read.

After the reading of the Charter, the Grand Patron will say:

G. P.—Sisters and Brothers, you have heard read the Charter granted to this Chapter. Do you accept it upon the conditions therein named?
ANS. . . . .
G. P.—My Sisters and Brothers, the duties and responsibilities which you now propose to assume are serious and important. We greatly rejoice at the organization of every new body of the Order of the Eastern Star, as it is another witness of the

truth long denied by prejudice and persecution, that women are able to keep a secret and govern or control an organized society.

To be constituted a Chapter of the Order of the Eastern Star is for all to take upon themselves new duties, and to enter into closer relations of interdependence. To perform those duties well requires constant effort, and a watchfulness over yourselves that never sleeps. When you are invested with the powers guaranteed by the Warrant of Constitution, you may so act as to win honor, or so as to incur disgrace. There should be a firm and fixed determination, and steady purpose of mind, on the part of each, that the labors of this Chapter shall be made interesting and instructive; that they shall not be confined to the mere ceremony of opening, closing, and conferring degrees, but shall be devoted to mutual instruction, to the cultivation of the social feelings and acts of kindness, and to the practice of an active and earnest beneficence.

Morally, the work of a Chapter of the Order of the Eastern Star extends far beyond mutual relief and assistance, and the ordinary ministrations of charity. The field of its exertions is not enclosed within the walls of a Chapter room, nor limited to the circle of its membership. That field is bounded by the realms of the whole society, and there is labor sufficiently extensive for us all.

With these views, but briefly expressing the mission and purposes of our association, we will now proceed with the services for which we are assembled. But first let us beseech our Heavenly Father to prosper this work and bless our labors with success. °°° (*calls up the Chapter*)

If the Chapter had already been opened before the Grand Officers entered, the Bible will be open upon the Altar, but if not, the G.P. will request the G. Con. to attend at the Altar, and then will say:

G.P.—Our Grand Chaplain will lead us in prayer.

PRAYER

GR. CHAP.—Father and Source of all things, Who art revealed unto us in the visible things of this universe—Thy Creation—be pleased to give unto us constancy and prudence, boldness and hope, a full faith and never-failing charity. Light with Thy presence this new temple which we now erect and constitute, and make it verily a holy house and a place where love and pure thoughts shall always dwell. Strengthen the hearts and illumine the souls of those who are of its household, and of the true and faithful everywhere; and so conduct their works and bless and prosper their laudable undertakings, that we and they shall not be found to have lived and labored in vain. Amen.

G. P.— ° (*seats the Chapter*).

G. P.—Brother Grand Marshal, let the members

of the Chapter about to be constituted, with their officers elect, form round the altar one of our revered symbols.

The Grand Marshal will place all the members of the new Chapter in the form of an equilateral triangle around the altar, with the apex at the East, all facing inward. When so arranged, he says:

G. M.—Grand Patron, the members of the new Chapter now about to be constituted are in order.

The Grand Patron calls up the Chapter, °°° *when the Grand Matron descends from the dais, and passes, with the Grand Chaplain, inside the triangle. The Grand officers and members of other chapters form, as near as the limits of the room will permit, a square around all. The Grand Chaplain will read the following passages of Scripture:*

G. C.—And Jephthah vowed a vow unto the Lord, and said, If Thou shalt without fail deliver the children of Ammon into my hands, then it shall be, that whatsoever cometh forth of the doors of my house to meet me, when I return in peace from the children of Ammon, shall surely be the Lord's, and I will offer it up for a burnt-offering. So Jephthah passed over unto the children of Ammon, and the Lord delivered them into his hands. Thus the children of Ammon were subdued before the children of Israel. And Jephthah came to Mizpeh unto his house, and behold, his daughter came out to meet him with timbrels and with dances. And it came to pass, when he saw her, that he rent his clothes, and said, "Alas, my daughter! thou hast brought me very low, and thou art one of them that trouble me; for I have opened my mouth unto the Lord, and I cannot go back."

And she said unto him, "My father, if thou hast opened thy mouth unto the Lord, do to me according to that which hath proceeded out of thy mouth; forasmuch as the Lord hath taken vengeance for thee on thine enemies, even of the children of Ammon."

And Ruth said, "Entreat me not to leave thee, or to return from following after thee; for whither thou goest, I will go: and where thou lodgest, I will lodge; thy people shall be my people, and thy God, my God. Where thou diest, will I die, and there will I be buried; the Lord do so to me, and more also, if aught but death part thee and me." And, behold, Boaz came from Bethlehem, and said unto the reapers, "The Lord be with you," and they answered, "The Lord bless thee." Then said Boaz unto his servant that was set over the reapers, "Whose damsel is this?"

Now it came to pass on the third day, that Esther put on her royal apparel, and stood in the inner court of the King's house; and the King sat upon his royal throne. And when the King saw Esther, the queen, standing in the court, she obtained favor in his sight; and the King held out to Esther the golden scepter that was in his hand. So Esther drew near, and touched the scepter. Then said the King unto her, "What wilt thou, Queen Esther? and what is thy request? it shall be even given thee even to the half of the kingdom."

Then Martha, as soon as she heard that Jesus was coming, went and met Him. Then said Martha unto Jesus, "Lord, if Thou hadst been here my brother had not died. But I know that even now, whatsoever Thou wilt ask of God, God will give it Thee." Jesus saith unto her, "Thy brother shall rise again." Martha saith unto Him, "I know that he shall rise again in the resurrection at the last day." Jesus saith unto her, "I am the resurrection and the life; he that believeth in me, though he were dead, yet shall he live; and whosoever liveth and believeth in me shall never die."

Grace be with you, mercy and peace, from God the Father. For the truth's sake, which dwelleth in us, and shall be with us forever. And now I beseech thee, lady, not as though I wrote a new commandment unto thee, but that which we had from the beginning, that we love one another.

After the reading, the Grand Matron will say:

G. M.—Sisters and Brothers, before the Grand Patron proceeds to constitute and inaugurate your

Chapter, I will receive your pledges of fidelity. These are entirely consistent with your former pledges as members of the Order of the Eastern Star.

1. Do you promise that you will bear true fealty and allegiance to the laws and regulations of the Grand Chapter, and the by-laws of the Chapter of which you may be a member?

ANS.—I will.

2. Do you promise that you will never be governed by personal animosities or prejudices in matters that relate to members of your body, or to other worthy members of the Order, or to sisters or brothers applying for admission into your Chapter?

ANS.—I will.

3. Do you promise that you will contribute, so far as may be in your power, to the general good of the Order, avoid disputes, quarrels, and evil speaking, and be kind and courteous to members of the society, wherever you meet them?

ANS.—I will.

G. M.—Repeat, then, with me:

All repeat as follows:

ALL—These are my sacred and solemn pledges, and I will truly and religiously keep them.

The Grand Patron continues the ceremony, and says:

G. P.—Almighty Father, Who art constantly manifesting Thyself to us by Thy works, receive graciously the profound homage that we pay to Thee, and permit us to consecrate to Thee this living temple which we are now about to constitute.

Take under Thy especial protection all those who shall be lawfully appointed to rule therein, that they may religiously comply with all the obligations by them contracted toward Thee, and toward all to whom they are bound by the bonds of duty.

Cause it to be that those who constitute this Chapter shall have but one heart, but one soul, to love, honor, and obey Thee, as Thy Infinite Beneficence requires; and to love each other as Thou lovest them.

Banish from this temple all evil passions, all prejudices, all intolerance. May we meet each other here, as the children of our Father, whose beneficent hand reaches all His children, and leads them by the same path to the gates of eternity.

And when the hand on Time's dial points to the last hour of our earthly labors, and the powers of life go away from us, help us to pass through the valley of the shadow of death, and lead us to that home wherein are peace and happiness for those who love and honor Thee and keep Thy commandments.

The Grand Chaplain will then give the following:

PRAYER

G. C.—Our gracious Father Who art in heaven, Who alone canst defend and protect us amid the manifold dangers that beset us in our journey through life; vouchsafe to us Thy powerful aid, we beseech Thee, in all our trials and temptations. Lay broad and deep in the hearts of the members of this new Chapter a knowledge of the responsibilities devolving upon them; that in the discharge of their various duties the loving spirit inculcated through the ceremonies of our Order may be more and more realized. Give to those whom we have placed in authority the spirit of equity, sincerity, courage, and wisdom, that they may govern with that prudence which well becometh a wise ruler. Give to those who must obey, wisdom and valor, justice and faithfulness, truth and honesty; to our enemies, forgiveness and brotherly kindness. Preserve us from all impatience and inordinate cares. Let us not be revengeful nor unthankful, nor envious and detracting; but enable us, by union, harmony, and zeal, to benefit our fellow-creatures. Amen.

ALL—Amen.

The Grand Officers and all others will resume their stations, when a suitable Ode may be sung.

The Grand Patron will then, with hands extended, say:

CONSTITUTING AND INAUGURATING 243

G. P.—In the name of our Heavenly Father, unto Whom be all honor and glory forever, and under the auspices of the Grand Chapter of the State of ......, Order of the Eastern Star, I do pronounce and declare this Chapter to be duly constituted and inaugurated, in ample form, under the distinctive name and title of ...... Chapter, No. ..., Order of the Eastern Star, in accordance with the terms of its Charter. I consecrate it as a living Temple to works of Charity and Beneficence, to the service of Truth, Virtue, and Harmony. May Peace, Unity, and Loving Kindness always reign in it. May it abundantly prosper, and all its undertakings be wise and good, and crowned with success.

A strain of triumphant music may be played. The Grand Patron says:

G. P.—Attention. Sisters and Brothers, give the grand honors.

G. P.— * We are now ready to install the officers of this Chapter.

The Chapter is called to order, and the installation of officers takes place. (For installation service, see p. 185.)

If the Grand Officers retire before the Chapter is closed, they will do so in the same manner as they entered.

DEDICATION OF EASTERN STAR HALL

These ceremonies may be performed by the officers of a Subordinate Chapter, but more properly by the officers of the Grand Chapter, under direction of the Grand Patron.

The room should be arranged as for the regular meetings of the Chapter, with the addition of an extra chair in the West, South, and North, and a pedestal or small table in each place, on which flowers may be placed and a banner suspended.

If the ceremonies are public and performed before an audience with strangers, the Chapter must be opened without passwords, signs, etc.

To make this ceremony impressive the following should be used: flowers, music, and appropriate banners (about 12 x 18 inches), on which should be inscribed the words: Peace (blue), Faith (green), Charity (white), Hope (green), Truth (red), Virtue (blue), Wisdom (red), Love (white).

When the Grand Officers conduct the ceremonies, they will assemble in an adjoining room, and form in procession in the following order:

Flag Bearers

Grand Marshal

Associate G. Conductress, carrying vessel with oil, and blue flowers.

Grand Electa

Grand Martha

Grand Lecturer

Grand Treasurer

Grand Trustee

Grand Trustee

Grand Conductress, carrying vessel with wine, and yellow flowers.

Grand Adah

Grand Ruth

Grand Esther

Grand Warder

Grand Secretary

Grand Trustee

Grand Musician

Associate Grand Matron, carrying vessel with corn and white flowers.

Associate Grand Patron

Grand Chaplain, carrying a Bible

Grand Matron, carrying vessel with salt and red flowers.

Grand Patron

The Grand Patron requests the Grand Conductress, who will be accompanied by the Grand Marshal, to inform the W. Matron that the Grand Officers are ready to dedicate the Hall to the uses of the Order of the Eastern Star. The Grand Conductress gives two raps at the door.

WARDER—Worthy Matron, there is an alarm at the door of the Chapter.

W. MATRON—Ascertain who makes the alarm, and report.

WAR.—(*Opening the door*). Who is it that knocks?

G. C.—The Grand Conductress of the Grand Chapter, who requests admittance for the purpose of communicating the order of the Grand Patron.

WAR.—(*Without closing the door*). Worthy Matron, the alarm was caused by the Grand Conductress of the Grand Chapter, who requests admittance for the purpose of communicating the orders of the Grand Patron.

W. M.—(*Calls up the Chapter*) ***. Let the Grand Conductress have free entrance.

The G. Conductress and G. Marshal advance to west of the Altar, when the former says:

G. COND.—Worthy Matron, officers and members of ...... Chapter, No. ...., I am directed by the Grand Patron of the Grand Chapter, Order of the Eastern Star, of the State of ......, to inform you that he and the other Grand Officers are ready to dedicate this Hall to the uses of the Order.

W. M.—Grand Conductress, please convey to the Grand Patron our thanks, and inform him that we are ready to receive the Grand Officers, and obey any orders he may be pleased to communicate to us.

The G. Cond. and G. Mar. retire, when she repeats to the Grand Patron the response of the W. Matron. The members remain standing, low, soft music being played. The Grand Patron says:

G. P.—The Chapter duly convened is prepared to receive us. Let us proceed to perform the duty for which we have assembled.

The door is thrown open, and the procession enters, passing to the right and left of the altar, outside of the star, facing the East; the Grand Patron and Grand Matron in the center, when all salute the Worthy Matron.[1]
The Matron invites the Grand Patron and Grand Matron to the East, where she hands the former the gavel. The grand honors[2] *are given by the Chapter, and the Matron says:*

W. M.—Grand Patron and Grand Matron, in behalf of ...... Chapter, No. ...., I bid you, and those who accompany you, a hearty welcome.

G. P.—Worthy Matron and members of ...... Chapter, we gratefully accept the generous welcome extended to us, and return our sincere acknowledgments for this courtesy. The Officers of ...... Chapter will vacate their stations and the Officers of the Grand Chapter will assume them. °

---

[1] *When the ceremonies are performed in public, only the public sign of salutation is given.*
[2] *Not in a public meeting. W.M. would introduce the Grand Matron and Grand Patron to the assembly.*

MUSIC

The Chapter is called to order. ° *When all are seated, the Worthy Matron will rise, and say:*

W. M.—Grand Patron, we greatly rejoice at your coming among us, and especially when you so kindly express a desire to set apart this hall to the sacred uses of our Order, and to dedicate it to the purposes of Benevolence and Loving Kindness.

G. P.—Worthy Matron, Sisters and Brothers, we congratulate you upon the completion of this beautiful hall, which we will, in accordance with your request, dedicate to those noble principles which should ever impel us to the cheerful performance of our duties; and to consecrate it to those cardinal virtues which adorn and elevate humanity. Within these walls, and beneath this roof, you are to assemble, from time to time, to assist and encourage each other in the great work laid out for you to do in the cause of Benevolence, Truth, and Love. Around this altar you are to cultivate and nourish those sweet flowers that Love scatters on the rugged pathway of human life. It is a well-established fact that none of us acts as nobly as we resolve, but we effect little when we do not aim at a mark higher than we can reach. We may, however, hope that our united efforts

DEDICATION

shall lead to the raising and spreading of the sublime principles of our Order throughout the world, and that wherever we may erect a temple, it shall be consecrated by the approval of the Supreme Grand Patron of the Universe, without Whose aid and blessing no work should be undertaken.

Sister Grand Chaplain, lead us in prayer as we invoke the blessing of Almighty God. * * *

PRAYER

G. CHAP.—Almighty God, receive graciously the profound homage that we pay to Thee, and permit us to consecrate to Thee this living temple. We would humbly draw near and beg Thy blessing on the work in which we are engaged. We pray Thee to take under Thy special protection all those who shall be lawfully appointed to rule therein, that they may religiously comply with all the obligations by them contracted toward Thee, and toward all to whom they are bound by the bonds of duty. Banish from this temple all evil passions, all prejudices, all intolerance. May we meet each other here as the children of one Father, Whose beneficent hand reaches all His children, and leads them by the same path to the gates of happiness. Forgive whatever is amiss in us, who have not the wisdom to do all things aright. Lead us in the path of righteousness, that our thoughts and deeds may redound to Thy greater glory and the good of our fellow-creatures. Amen.

ALL—Amen.

The following, or some other suitable Ode, may be sung:

> Thou hast Thy temple, Lord of all,
> Where'er Thy light and glory shine;
> While suns and stars before Thee fall,
> And own Thy majesty divine.
>
> Lord! in Thy sight completed stands
> This temple to Thy truth and grace;
> And now we lift our hearts and hands
> To Thee, to consecrate the place.
>
> Lord! in our hearts Thy kingdom build
> That they may living temples be,
> That with Thy faith and comfort filled,
> We may each day live nearer Thee.

G. P.— * (*seats the Chapter*).

The Grand Matron will rise in her station and say:

G. M.—"I was glad when they said unto me, Let us go into the house of the Lord. Our feet shall stand within thy gates, O Jerusalem! Pray for the peace of Jerusalem; they shall prosper that love thee. Peace be within thy walls, and prosperity within thy palaces. For my brethren and companions' sakes, I will now say, Peace be within thee."

DEDICATION

The Associate Grand Matron will rise and say:

A. G. M.—"For the Lord hath chosen Zion; He hath desired it for His habitation. Lift up your hands in the sanctuary, and bless the Lord, ye that stand in the house of the Lord, in the courts of the house of God. The Lord that made heaven and earth, bless thee out of Zion."

The Grand Conductress will rise and say:

G. C.—"I rejoice at the things that were said unto me: We shall go into the house of the Lord. Our feet are standing in thy courts, O Jerusalem. Because of the house of the Lord our God, we have sought good things for thee. Let peace be in thy strength, and abundance in thy towers; for the sake of my companions, I speak peace for thee."

The Associate Grand Conductress will rise and say:

A. G. C.—"Unless the Lord build the house, they labor in vain that build it. Unless the Lord keep the city, he watcheth in vain that keepeth it. Blessed are they that dwell in Thy house. For He showeth us good things, and the light of His countenance is shed upon us."

The Associate Grand Patron, standing in the West, will say:

A. G. P.—"The earth is the Lord's, and the fullness thereof; the world, and they that dwell therein. For He hath founded it upon the seas, and established it upon the floods. Who shall ascend into the hill of the Lord? and who shall stand in His holy place? He that hath clean hands and a pure heart; who hath not lifted up his soul unto vanity, nor sworn deceitfully. He shall receive the blessing from the Lord, and righteousness from the God of his salvation. Lift up your heads, O ye gates, and be ye lifted up, ye everlasting doors; and the King of Glory shall come in. Who is this King of Glory? The Lord, strong and mighty, the Lord, mighty in battle. Lift up your heads, O ye gates; even lift them up, ye everlasting doors; and the King of Glory shall come in. Who is this King of Glory? The Lord of hosts, He is the King of Glory."

The Grand Patron will rise and say:

G. P.—The special duty to which this evening is assigned, and for which we are assembled, is the Dedication of this hall to the uses of the Order of the Eastern Star. The honorable and exalted purposes of our Order are established upon the principles of Benevolence and Loving Kindness, in our respect for the binding force of a vow, in our devotion to religious principles, in our fidelity to kindred and friends, in our undeviating faith in the hour of trial, and in our patience and submission under wrongs. The ceremony of Dedication will now begin.

The following, or other appropriate verse may be sung:

Music—*Bring Flowers*

How brilliantly streams, from the vaults above,
The drapery gemmed by the God of love!
Then hither bring, from your stores of light,
A banner of radiance pure and bright,
That unnumbered rays may our work illume,
And a glory reveal in the mystic room.

The Associate Grand Conductress, standing in her place in the North, pours oil upon the floor, and says:

A. G. C.—In the name of our Father, Who is in heaven, I consecrate this hall to PEACE.

At this moment she displays a small banner, on which is the word PEACE, *and suspends it on pedestal at her station; she continues:*

May Peace and Contentment forever reign within these walls. May the oil of joy and the flowers of peace give gladness to the hearts of all who assemble here. Glory be unto God in the highest, and on earth peace and good will to men.

G. CHAP.—"Behold, how good and how pleasant it is for brethren to dwell together in unity; for there the Lord commanded the blessing, even life for evermore."

The following, or other verse may be sung:

Music—*Bring Flowers*

How charmingly glow, in the hours of May,
The roses and violets, blest array!
Then hither bring, from the painted fields,
All the gems that o'er-bounteous nature yields;
Then unnumbered hues may our work approve,
And a touch of the flow'ry time float above.

The Grand Conductress will rise, pour wine upon the floor, and say:

G. C.—In the name of the heroines of the Order, I consecrate this hall to CHARITY.

Displays a banner on which is inscribed the word CHARITY, *which she will suspend, and continues:*

May the members of the Order, wherever located, ever labor to assist the needy, comfort the suffering, and cheer the disconsolate with the wine of contentment and the flowers of plenty.

G. CHAP.—"Though I speak with the tongues of men and of angels, and have not charity, I am become as sounding brass or a tinkling cymbal; charity never faileth."

The following, or other verse may be sung:

Music—*Bring Flowers*

How beauteously shows, on a happy face,
The smiling of innocence, truth of grace;
Then hither bring, with a sweet content,

Every joyous look that the heart hath lent,
Then unnumbered smiles may our work attend
Nor a sigh nor a tear with the pleasure blend.

The Associate Grand Matron, standing in her place, scatters wheat on the floor, and says:

A. G. M.—In the name of the Grand Chapter, I consecrate this hall to TRUTH.

Displays a banner on which is inscribed the word TRUTH, *which she suspends, and continues:*

May the good seed and the fragrant flowers here sown, like the grain sown in the earth, spring up an hundred fold for future use and blessings; and may Truth, that ennobling virtue, which lies at the foundation of all other virtues, ever govern the members of this Chapter.

G. CHAP.—"He that walketh uprightly and worketh righteousness, and speaketh the truth in his heart, O Lord, shall abide in Thy tabernacle, and shall dwell in Thy holy hill."

The following, or other verse may be sung:

MUSIC—*Bring Flowers*

How solemnly rise, from the soul in care,
The burdens of pity, of love, and prayer!
Then hither bring, with a faith on fire,
Such a prayer of o'erpowering strong desire,
That unnumbered angels our work may grace
And a touch of God's glory pervade the place.

The Grand Matron, standing in the East, scatters salt on the floor, and says:

G. M.—As salt was an emblem of hospitality, friendship and fidelity among the people of antiquity, I scatter this symbol over the floor of this hall as a pledge of unbounded hospitality to those who partake, and in a belief that the Chapter meeting here will be devoted to the peaceful pursuits which characterize our Order. Therefore, in the name of the whole Order, I consecrate this hall to WISDOM.

Displays a banner on which is inscribed the word WISDOM, *which being suspended, she continues:*

May all the deliberations of this Chapter, when assembled in this place, be governed by WISDOM; may it prosper, and all its labors be crowned with success; may the actions and motives of its members be as pure as new fallen snow upon the imperial mountains, and may peace be evermore in the hearts of all who enter this hall. Brighter than the bow of the Covenant, bent in the East after refreshing showers, be forever our covenant with each other.

GR. CHAP.—"Wisdom hath builded her house; she hath hewn it out of her seven pillars. She hath sent forth her maidens; she crieth upon the highest places of the city, at the gates, at the coming in at the doors. The Lord possessed me in the beginning of His way before His works of old. When He prepared the heavens, I was there; when He set a compass upon the face of the depth. Blessed is the man that heareth me, watching daily at my gates, waiting at the posts of my doors."

The following, or other verse may be sung:
Music—*Bring Flowers*

Bring flowers to the shrine where we kneel in prayer,
They are nature's offering, their place is there!
They speak of hope to the fainting heart,
With a voice of promise they come and part,
They sleep in dust through the wintry hours,
They break forth in glory; bring flowers, bright flowers.

G. P. °°° *calls the Chapter up. Grand Officers leave their places, bringing with them the vessels and articles of consecration, and surround the altar; the Grand Patron on the East, with the Grand Chaplain on his left, and the Grand Matron on his right, who holds a banner on which is inscribed the word Love; the A. G. Matron on the West of the altar, with the banner Virtue; the A. G. Patron to her left; the G. Cond., with the banner Hope, on the South; the A. G. Cond., with the banner Faith, on the North; the other Grand Officers on the North and South of the altar. The Grand Officers thus stationed, the Grand Patron will say:*

G. P.—In the name of Loving Kindness, which

is the spirit and soul of all true religion; in the name of Truth, which is omnipotent and eternal; in the name of Faith and Hope, the two chief blessings bestowed by Providence on humanity; in the name of Virtue and Love, I dedicate this hall to the uses of the Order of the Eastern Star.

When the words FAITH *and* HOPE *are uttered, the Grand Cond. and Associate Gr. Cond. will lay their banners upon the Altar; so when the words* VIRTUE *and* LOVE *are spoken, the Grand Matron and Associate G. M. will lay their banners upon the Altar. When the word* DEDICATE *is uttered, the four officers will, simultaneously, pour the elements of consecration upon the floor. The Grand Patron continues:*

May the Beneficence of the Order here fall like soft rain upon parched places, comforting and consoling the hearts of the afflicted as the dews of heaven nourish and gladden the green leaves, giving new life and sweeter fragrance to thirsting flowers.

The G. M., A. G. M., G. C., and A. G. C. will here strew flowers on and around the altar. The Grand Patron continues:

And may we so live, and perform the duties that God requires of us here, and when we lie down to our last sleep in the narrow grave, His angels may crown our souls with sweet flowers, freshly gathered from the lawns of Paradise.

(MUSIC)

The Grand Officers will return to their respective stations.

PRAYER

GR. CHAP.—Our Father Who art in heaven, we beseech Thee to bless the work in which we have been engaged. Let the lessons we have received sink deeply into our hearts, so that this shall have been to us no idle ceremony, but a means of edification in righteousness and truth and love. May we all leave this place with our good resolutions strengthened, our charities enlarged, and our hearts expanded in all-embracing love. Bless, O Heavenly Father, the Order of which we are members. Aid us in the good work of Benevolence to which we are pledged, and give success to our efforts. Bless this edifice in the promotion of the good objects to which it has this day been set apart. Let Thy protecting care be over all those who here shall meet together. Make them faithful to their duties, and zealous in every good word and work. And unto Thee, our God and Father, be ascribed glory, and dominion, and power, world without end. Amen.

ALL—Amen.

PROCLAMATION

G. P.—The Grand Marshal will proclaim the dedication of this hall and the services completed.

G. Mar. goes to the East, ascends the dais; G. P. hands him the gavel.

G. MAR.—By order of the Grand Patron of the Order of the Eastern Star, of the State of ......, I proclaim this hall regularly and constitutionally dedicated to the uses of the Order, and the dissemination of the principles of Benevolence and all good works. *

G. Mar. returns to station.

G. P.—Sisters and Brothers, I feel convinced, from the interest you have manifested in our proceedings, that the good effect of the imposing ceremonies of this occasion has not been lost upon your hearts. In setting apart this hall for the noble purposes just proclaimed, we have renewed our vows to practice the sublime lessons of our Order. May this building be more permanent than Roman palaces and Grecian temples, and, so long as its foundations stand, may it be devoted to the benefit of humanity. Within its walls let Benevolence be continually inculcated and practiced. Here may the wise and gentle teachings of our Society bear rich fruit, and may the rosy splendors of Loving Kindness illume the souls of those who surround this Altar with strength and courage, manfully facing the storms and disasters of life; helping and being helped; blessing and being blessed, in turn.

Sisters and Brothers of .... Chapter, we now finally deliver into your hands this beautiful temple. Joy be within its courts, and Peace a constant guest. May these walls never echo with the sound of any angry or an unkind word. May all the influences that flow hence be good, and for good now and forever.

G. P.—(*gives with gavel*) *.

G. P.—The Officers of the Grand Chapter will vacate their stations and the Officers of ...... Chapter will resume them.

Regular business of the Chapter is then continued.

CHAPTER OF SORROW

It is earnestly recommended that each Chapter of the Eastern Star devote one meeting each year (to be specified in the By-laws) to a Chapter of Sorrow to pay respect to any member of the Grand Chapter, or any member of that Chapter, who has passed on during the year.

The following suggestions are offered as a guide and may be elaborated upon or simplified as desired:

Altar and officers' pedestals draped in black; an urn placed on the Altar and covered with a black cloth; white flowers and ferns laid upon the Altar; white candles on the desks of Treasurer and Secretary; if the deceased was an officer, her jewel of office may be laid upon the Altar; members wear mourning badges; a five pointed floral piece on the Patron's pedestal, consisting of blue, yellow, white, green, and red flowers and ferns; appropriate vocal and instrumental selections.

Such services need not be private and may be held in the presence of non-members of the Order. However, if held during a regular Chapter meeting, the Star Points, Marshal, and Conductresses may retire from the room when the Matron will instruct them to do so in order that they may prepare for draping the Altar. On re-entering the room, the Marshal would lead, then the Conductresses, next Electa and Adah holding two corners of a black or purple altar cloth and Martha and Esther holding the other two corners. Ruth would follow them carrying a sheaf of wheat in each hand. With dim lights and appropriate music the altar cloth would be silently dropped over the Altar and the officers then take their regular stations.

OPENING THE CHAPTER

The officers being in their places, and the assemblage seated, the Patron will call up the Chapter (***), and say:

W. P.—Sisters and Brothers, the brevity and uncertainty of human life will now afford us subjects for contemplation. Let us for a little while vary the ordinary pursuits of our Chapter, from the consideration of those heroines whose histories light up the sacred pages with such a warmth of color. Let us turn to the names and memories of those Sisters and Brothers[1] who have fallen in life's battle during the past year, acknowledged the supremacy of death, grounded their arms before a victor whom none can resist, and entered upon

---

[1] *The language must, in all cases, be varied to suit the particular circumstance.*

the sleep that knows no waking. Recommending these sentiments to your earnest consideration, and soliciting your assistance in the solemn ceremonies about to take place, I declare this Chapter of Sorrow opened.

The Chaplain or Patron will then deliver the following or some other suitable

PRAYER

Almighty and merciful God, infinite in wisdom and goodness, extend to us the riches of Thy everlasting favor; make us grateful for the benefits we now enjoy, and crown us with immortal life and honor. Thou hast decreed that we all shall die and come to dust. But Thou hast also decreed that we shall rise from death to everlasting life. In such a faith may we live, ever remembering that here we have no abiding-place. In such a faith may we die, ever believing that, when our earthly house is dissolved, we may be welcomed to that glorious mansion not made with hands, eternal in the heavens. Aid these mourning friends to feel that the ties of kindred, affection, and friendship are not broken by the power of death, and that the family in heaven and on earth are still the same. Forgive our transgressions; aid us in our duties; comfort us in our sorrows; and take us, at last, unto Thyself in heaven. Amen.

Will then be sung the following, or some other appropriate

HYMN

I Would Not Live Alway

I would not live alway; I ask not to stay
Where storm after storm rises dark o'er the way.
The few lurid mornings that dawn on us here
Are enough for life's woes, full enough for its cheer.

I would not live alway; thus fetter'd by sin,
Temptation without, and corruption within;
E'en the rapture of pardon is mingled with fears,
And the cup of thanksgiving with penitent tears.

I would not live alway; no, welcome the tomb,
Since Jesus hath lain there, I dread not its gloom.
There, sweet be thy rest, till He bid me arise
To hail Him in triumph ascending the skies.

Who, who would live alway, away from his God,
Away from yon heaven, that blissful abode!
Where the rivers of pleasure flow o'er the bright plains,
And the noontide of glory eternally reigns.

Where the saints of all ages in harmony meet,
Their Saviour and brethren, transported to greet;
While the anthems of rapture unceasingly roll,
And the smile of the Lord is the feast of the soul.

W. P.—The departed answer not to our call. Once they lived and labored; but now their Star is set on this world, and they have passed into the light that is beyond the valley of the Shadow of Death. In vain we call upon them here. We shall no more hear their voice until we also have awakened in another world. Let us, however, not mourn like those that have no hope. He who created us and surrounded us with manifold blessings in the present life, and gave us capacities for far greater things in the life to come, will not forget to be merciful to us when we shall stand before His throne, and will connect again the chain of friendship so painfully broken here.

Sister Worthy Matron, what duties of Adoptive Masonry have we now to perform?

W. M.—The last offices of Sisterhood and Loving-kindness—to pay honors to the memory of the departed; for death has come among us, to cut off the young with the aged whom we love. They fall alike, as the ripe and the unripe fruit, and there is none to gather them up.

W. P.—They have gone but a little sooner than we to the silent land. Sister Associate Matron, your place in our Chapter of Sorrow is in the West. What is your duty there?

A. M.—To teach my Sisters and Brothers the brevity and uncertainty of human life, and the instability of human fortune. For the children of this earthly tabernacle pass away as the dew of the morning, as the drops of the shower that linger upon the grass.

W. P.—Sister Conductress, your place in our Chapter of Sorrow is in the South. What is your duty there?

COND.—To teach my Sisters and Brothers that it is not all of life to live; but that the Great Master of Life hath promised us an opportunity to serve Him in the world where faith is lost in sight, and hope ends in fruition.

W. P.—Sister Associate Conductress, your place in our Chapter of Sorrow is in the North. What is your duty there?

ASSOC. COND.—To teach my Sisters and Brothers that out of the darkness of the grave spring the most glowing hopes of immortality. For the Lord redeemeth the souls of His servants; and none of them that trust in Him shall be desolate.

W. P.—Sister Treasurer, your place in our Chapter of Sorrow is in the Northeast. What is your duty there?

TREAS.—To teach my Sisters and Brothers that the true riches of life are those that we are permitted to bear with us to the heavenly world, the treasure of good deeds.

W. P.—Sister Secretary, your place in our Chapter of Sorrow is in the Southeast. What is your duty there?

SEC.—To teach my Sisters and Brothers that the brightest record we can make in the present life is the obedience we render to our Father in heaven, by serving Him and keeping His commandments.

W. P.—Sisters Adah, Ruth, Esther, Martha, and Electa, it is your part collectively to display in our midst the mystical Star of Adoptive Masonry. In our Chapter of Sorrow, what are your duties?

ADAH—My duty is to point hopefully to the blue expanse, beyond which lie the happy homes of our departed.

RUTH—My duty is to point to the golden tints of sunset, emblematical of the peaceful deathbed of those who sweetly sleep in the Lord.

ESTHER—My duty is to point to the pure robes of the saints as indicative of the spotless inheritance reserved for those who live in the faith of the one ever living God.

MARTHA—My duty is to point to the verdure of God's evergreen trees as symbolical of the unfading glories of the heavenly groves.

ELECTA—My duty is to point to the rosy tints of sunrise, as promising a blissful resurrection to those who die in the Lord.

W. P.—Sister Warder, your station in our Chapter of Sorrow is within the door. What is your duty there?

WARDER—To teach my Sisters and Brothers

that no watch or ward can prevent the entrance of the King of Terrors to our midst.

W. P.—Sisters and Brothers, these lessons must not be lightly treated. Healing and profit must be drawn from our sorrows. It is the work of stupid, unreflecting minds to close our hearts against the warnings of Death. Our Divine Master admonishes us, "Be ye also ready."

Sister Secretary, will you read the names of those who have departed during the past year and for whom we meet tonight to pay our respects.

The Secretary now reads the list, previously prepared, of the fraternal dead of the preceding year, dwelling upon the facts of association in this Chapter; the official positions held, if any; the time and place of burial, etc. If obituary notices have been prepared for any of the deceased, eulogies, either in prose or verse, or any other forms of commemoration, they should be read immediately after calling the names, respectively, by the Secretary; and, being read, should be ordered on file among the records of the Chapter. These proceedings being had, the ceremonies of the Chapter of Sorrow will be continued.

HYMN

Friend after friend departs:
  Who hath not lost a friend?
There is no union here of hearts,
  That finds not here an end.
Were this frail world our only rest,
Living or dying, none were blest.

There is a world above
  Where parting is unknown—
A whole eternity of love
  And blessedness alone;
And faith beholds the dying here
Translated to that happier sphere.

If time and circumstances will admit, Funeral Eulogy of a general character, may be delivered by some member appointed at a previous meeting.

The Chaplain or Patron will then give the following, or some other suitable, prayer:

PRAYER

O Merciful and Loving Father, who hath made our present life but temporary, and thus decreed that the sorrows we endure shall not be perpetual, we thank Thee for the consciousness which Thou hast implanted in us that Thou dost exist and that the grave is not the end of life. Pity and forgive the errors of the living, so that the evil consequences of sin may not follow them into the other world. May we endure the crosses of life patiently as resting in hope of a blissful reward. And may we so labor upon the instructive designs of our Order that charity, friendship, good counsel, and morality may animate all our doings and render us well pleasing in Thy sight. Amen.

The Patron, taking the Floral Star in hand, advances near the altar, uncovers the Urn, and says:

W. P.—This Floral emblem of the Eastern Star, wrought in Nature's own hues and from her own materials, instructs us with an eloquence only known to stars, and flowers, and gems. Who does not love flowers? they not only please the eye and gratify the sense, but they are monitors of truth and righteousness. Flowers are the smiles of nature, and earth would be but a desert without them.

In the ritual of our Society flowers bear an important part. They suggest through their colors, and fragrance, and matchless forms, the brave lessons and womanly graces of the five heroines of the Eastern Star. It is proper, therefore, that in this our most solemn ceremonial we should introduce our traditional flowers with their appropriate lessons, and I shall call upon the immediate representatives of those heroines to evolve the lessons they contain.

Sister Adah, draw from these mute monitors of truth that portion of the Floral Star which suggests your particular place and impart to us its signification. (*He hands her the Floral Star.*)

ADAH—(*Plucks the blue flower from the Star and holds it up.*) Its lesson, my friends, is *Undying Love*. There are many who believe that the souls of our departed friends return, at times, when yearning love is strong within them, and bring us consolation from heavenly sources; others that our Divine Father makes His messengers of such, to save us from despair in those moments when our hearts sink within us. In the belief that true love is undying, I deposit this flower within the Urn of Remembrance. (*She does so, and then returns the Star to the Patron.*)

> W. P.—Blessed be God for flowers!
> For the bright, gentle, holy thoughts that breathe
> From out their odorous beauty, like a wreath
> Of sunshine, on life's hours!

Sister Ruth, continue these lessons; select that portion of the Floral Star which suggests your particular place and impart to us its signification. (*He hands her the Star.*)

RUTH—(*Plucks the yellow flower from the Floral Star and holds it up.*) Its lesson, my friends, is *Unending Possession*. We believe, upon highest authority, that it is only what we *have given* that abides with us when earthly treasures pass away.

CHAPTER OF SORROW

Believing this, we lay our beloved ones in the grave, trusting them to the hands of Him Who can never forfeit the guardianship of our jewels. In the belief that true love is unending, I deposit this flower within the Urn of Remembrance. (*She does so, and then returns the Star to the Patron.*)

W. P.—Yes, flowers have words: God gave to each
    A language of its own,
And bade the simple blossom teach,
    Where'er its seeds are sown.
His voice is on the mountain's height,
    And by the river's side,
Where flowers blush in glowing light,
    In Lowliness or Pride;
We feel, o'er all the blooming sod,
It is the language of our God.

Sister Esther, select that portion of the Floral Star which is suggestive of your place and impart to us its signification.

ESTHER—(*Plucks the white flower from the Floral Star and holds it up.*) Its lesson, my friends, is *Heart Purity*. A promise of ineffable consolation was once made, amidst the lilies on the mountainside, "Blessed are the pure in heart, for they shall see God!" Believing this, the humble may look up —the lowly may hope—for the Unerring Eye will detect them amidst the flowers of His field and they shall not fail to realize His promise: "Come, ye blessed of my Father, inherit the kingdom!" In the belief that no word of God can be lost, I deposit this flower within the Urn of Remembrance. (*She does so, and then returns the Star to the Patron.*)

W. P.—We thank Thee, Lord, for weal and woe,
    And whatsoe'er the trial be;
  'Twill serve to wean us from below
    And bring our spirits nigher Thee.

Sister Martha, select that portion of the Floral Star which is suggestive of your place and impart to us its signification.

MARTHA—(*Plucks the green sprig from the Floral Star and holds it up.*) Its lesson, my friends, is *Undeviating Sincerity*. They whose souls have been touched with celestial fire can know no change. Coldness may wound them, but they cannot be alienated. Absence only increases their devotion to Him who has won their hearts by His divine favor. As from the grave, ofttimes, the sweetest floweret springs, so from the anguish of death are born the richest proofs of undeviating sincerity. In the belief that true love is ever sincere, I deposit this green sprig within the Urn of Remembrance. (*She does so, and then returns the Star to the Patron.*)

W. P.—Shall we be left abandoned in the dust
    When Fate relenting lets the flower revive?
  Shall nature's voice, to man alone unjust,
    Bid him; though doomed to perish, hope to live?

CHAPTER OF SORROW 275

It is for this, fair Virtue oft must strive
With disappointment, penury, and pain?
No; heaven's immortal spring shall yet arrive,
And man's majestic beauty bloom again
Bright through the eternal year of love's triumphant reign!

Sister Electa, select your portion of the Floral Star, which is suggestive of your place, and impart to us its signification.

ELECTA—(*Plucks the Red flower from the Floral Star and holds it up.*) Its lesson, my friends, is *Unfading Beauty*. On the banks of the pure river of the water of life, clear as crystal, is the tree of life, which yieldeth her fruit every month. There is no night there, neither sun nor moon; for the glory of God doth lighten all the blissful place. Perfectly beautiful are the faces of the redeemed there; for they see the face of God and His name is in their foreheads. In the belief that true love is eternally beautiful, I deposit this flower within the Urn of Remembrance. (*She does so, and then returns the Star to the Patron.*)

W. P.—How instructive are these lessons! love undying and unending, animating hearts that are pure and sincere, will inherit the unfading beauty of which the Holy Spirit hath spoken. In this belief I deposit what remains of the Floral Star in the Urn of Remembrance. (*He does so, replacing the pall.*) Rent and torn and concealed from view by the dark pall enclosing it in, it recalls the image of those whose death has rent from us, tearing our hearts with grief and concealing them from our eyes as by the pall of the grave! But blessed be God the Restorer, this concealment is but for a little. They shall come forth as the flowers in the spring and clothed with new beauty. Divulging all the secrets of the grave they shall come forth. Conquerors over the utmost power of death they shall come forth. A voice which they can in no wise resist shall summon them; a hand shall be stretched forth to strengthen them; and at once, all for which we sighed and wept and sorely regretted shall be restored to us in the Land where there is no night.

The Patron and Sisters return to their places, and the Patron continues the services.

The duty we owed to the dead is performed. It remains, that we who are alive should so live, and by our actions attend the coming of the day of fate, that we may neither be surprised, nor leave our duties imperfect, nor our sins uncanceled, nor our persons unreconciled, nor God unappeased; but that, when our bodies in their turn descend to their graves, our souls may ascend to the regions of eternal light. Whatever fate is to befall us in this world, let the motto of our lives be—for the *Past*, CHARITY; for the *Present*, HOPE; for the *Future*, FAITH.

CLOSING

W. P.—Sister Associate Matron, the labors of this Chapter of Sorrow being ended, it is proper that it be now closed. Make due announcement to the Sisters and Brothers, and invite them to assist.

ASSOC. M.—Sisters and Brothers, the labors of this Chapter of Sorrow being ended, it is the pleasure of the Worthy Patron that it be now closed.

HYMN

Air—*Joyfully, Joyfully*

Life is a vapor, how brief is its stay,
Vanishing, vanishing, passing away!
Life is a flower that springs in the morn,
Fading, ah, fading, no more to return.
Life is an arrow, how swift is its flight!
Life is the rose-tint that fades into night:
Lord! may our lives to Thy service be given,
Fading on earth but immortal in heaven.

Teach us the worth of the vanishing time,
Make every life in its purpose sublime;
Virtue and innocence, charity's dower,
Father of blessings, oh, grant us with power!
Patient and strong to endure to the end:
Hopeful and faithful and true to each friend;
Lord! may our lives to Thy service be given,
Fading on earth, but immortal in heaven.

The Chaplain will pronounce the following:

BENEDICTION

May the blessing of our Father, Who is in heaven, rest upon us all, now and forevermore! May friendship and love increase among us, and the remembrance of our friends who have gone away from among us make more dear unto us those who remain! The peace and blessing of Almighty God descend upon us and abide forever! Amen.

RESPONSE—So mote it be.

W. P.—This Chapter of Sorrow is now closed.

BURIAL SERVICE

GENERAL DIRECTIONS

1. No Sister (or Brother) can be buried with the formalities of the Order, unless it be at her own request, or that of her family, communicated to the Patron or Matron of the Chapter.

2. The Patron or Matron having received notice of the death of a sister, issues an order to the Secretary to notify the Chapter.

3. If the deceased was a Grand or Past Grand officer, it is proper to invite the officers of the Grand Chapter. The highest male Grand officer present may be asked to conduct the Burial Service.

4. Dark clothes to be worn. Mourning badges or a black crepe rosette to be worn on the left breast—for an elderly person; for a young person, white and black crepe.

5. A floral star, about fifteen inches from point to point, to be used in the service, the points to be of appropriately colored flowers; the crown of the star of immortelles, with a tuberose in the centre, and so constructed that the several points may be separated or drawn from the body of the star.

6. This service may be performed in a church or at the house of the deceased, with proper change of language.

7. The members will assemble at the Chapter room and go to the house of the deceased, or directly to the house, as most convenient.

8. The members of the Chapter will form a square

round the grave: the Patron at the head of the grave, with the Matron, Treasurer, Associate Conductress, and members on the right; the Associate Matron, Conductress, Secretary, and members on the left; Adah, Esther, and Electa on the right; Ruth, Martha, and Warder on the left of the grave; the mourners at the foot of the grave, inside of the square.

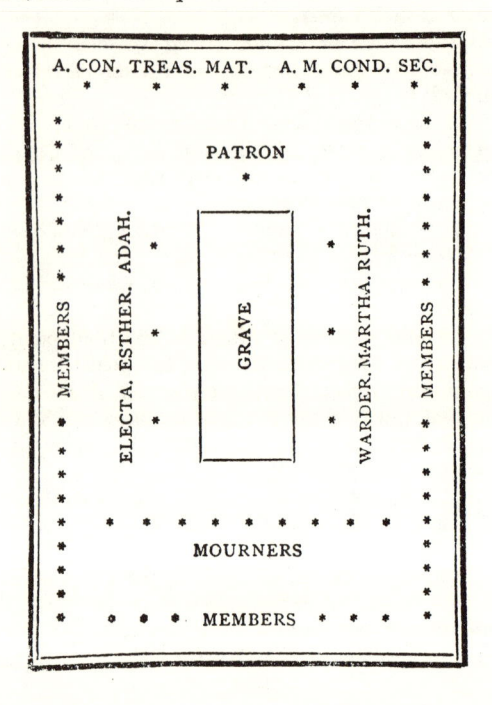

```
+-------------------------------------------------+
|  A. CON.  TREAS.  MAT.    A. M.  COND.  SEC.    |
|                                                 |
|                   PATRON                        |
|                                                 |
|      ELECTA. ESTHER. ADAH.   WARDER. MARTHA. RUTH. |
|  MEMBERS        |  GRAVE  |              MEMBERS |
|                                                 |
|                  MOURNERS                       |
|                  MEMBERS                        |
+-------------------------------------------------+
```

The foregoing arrangements being completed, the Patron will commence the services by saying:

PATRON—Friends, we are now assembled around the final resting-place of these mortal remains to perform those final rites and solemn duties of respect we owe to our departed Sister. A few reflections, therefore, applicable to the solemnities of this occasion, instructive and impressive as they should be to the living, may, with propriety, be offered on this sacred spot—a spot hallowed with the memories of departed friendships, which linger round the heart, awakening a thousand melancholy, yet pleasing reflections.

How wisely and appropriately it has been said that it is better to go to the house of mourning than to go to the house of feasting.

We are often told that in the world of matter all bodies are subject to the laws of mutual attraction and repulsion. The stars that fill the vault of heaven, the drops that make the ocean, the atoms that form the universe, are all controlled by a simple but mysterious power that renders the perfect isolation of even a grain of sand impossible. No human being can pass away into death without the knowledge or sympathy of some one. We cannot, if we would, live or die wholly unto ourselves. An individual may fall unseen, unwept, unhonored, and unsung, but when he drops like a pebble into the ocean of eternity, a ripple is created which must forever widen towards the limitless shore.

Our Heavenly Father hath again reminded us of the brevity and uncertainty of human life, and hath warned us also to be ready for that day which comes at last unto all, when the body returns to dust, and the spirit unto Him Who gave it.

Again, our heads are bowed down and our hearts are heavy. The lesson of the present is full of deep and significant meaning. Our beloved Sister has fallen in life's battle, acknowledged the supremacy of death, yielded to a victor, whom none can resist, and entered upon the sleep that knows no waking. Her star is set on this world, and she has passed into the light that is beyond the valley of the shadow of death. With her we have traveled the pilgrimage of life; with her we have sympathized in its vicissitudes and trials. She is now removed beyond the reach of human praise or censure. That we loved her, our presence here evinces. As she in her life exemplified the virtues of those chosen servants of God—the lovely heroines of the Order—so surely shall be her reward. The lessons of her exemplary life and many virtues linger in our remembrance, and their shining luster is reflected beyond the portals of the tomb.

Sisters, Brothers, and Friends, let us improve the remaining brief period of life, and be prepared to obey our heavenly Grand Patron's call from our

BURIAL SERVICE

labors on earth to everlasting happiness in the world to come.

Let us pray.

The Chaplain or Associate Matron, or a person appointed for the purpose, will read the following, or give, extemporaneously, some appropriate

PRAYER

O merciful and loving Father, Who hath made our present life but temporary, and thus decreed that the sorrows we endure shall not be perpetual; we thank Thee for the conciousness which Thou hast implanted in us that Thou dost exist, and that the grave is not the end of life. Pity and forgive the errors of the living, so that the evil consequences of sin may not follow them into the other world. May we endure the trials of life patiently, as resting in hope of a blissful reward. And may we so labor upon the instructive designs of our Order that Charity, Friendship, Good Counsel, and Morality may animate all our doings, purify our thoughts, and render us pleasing and acceptable in Thy sight. Amen.

After the Prayer, the members of the Order will join in singing the following, or some other appropriate

ADOPTIVE RITE RITUAL

HYMN

I would not live al-way; I ask not to stay,

Where storm af-ter storm ris-es dark o'er the way;

The few lu-rid mornings that dawn on us here

Are e-nough for life's woes, full e-nough for its cheer.

Who, who would live alway, away from his God;
Away from yon heaven, that blissful abode
Where the rivers of pleasure flow o'er the bright plains,
And the noontide of glory eternally reigns.

Where the saints of all ages in harmony meet,
Their Saviour and brethren, transported to greet;
While the anthems of rapture unceasingly roll,
And the smile of the Lord is the feast of the soul.

After singing, the Patron takes a Floral Star from the coffin (which should be prepared for the occasion, made five-pointed, and of the five appropriate colors. The coffin is lowered into the grave, after which the Patron proceeds as follows:

PATRON—This floral emblem of the Eastern Star, wrought in Nature's own hues and from her own materials, instructs us with an eloquence more powerful than words. Flowers are sensibly an antidote to the gloomy surroundings of death, and lend to the departed one the appearance of being asleep only; on the grave they are sweetly consoling; they tell that the buried one is not neglected; that her memory has not departed from the hearts of the sorrowing ones. They are the constant and living witnesses that there is a hope and a future life. They, like ourselves, fade, wither, and decay, yet, in the spring-tide of the resurrection, return to life, and in the celestial garden, where are collected God's choicest creation, with those who die in the Lord, shall blossom and flourish with the fragrance of supernal grace. Therefore, let them always adorn the coffin and bloom on the grave, for they are of heavenly appearance, and they tell of heavenly things.

In the ceremonies of our Order, flowers bear an important part. They are the beautiful silent hymns in which we read of the Creator's love to us, and suggest, through their colors and fragrance and matchless forms, the brave lessons and womanly graces of the Five Heroines of the Eastern Star. It is proper, therefore, that in this, our most solemn ceremonial, we should introduce our traditional flowers, with their appropriate lessons; and I now call upon the immediate representatives of those Heroines to remind us of the lessons they contain.

Sister Adah, draw from these mute monitors of truth that portion of the Floral Star which suggests your particular duty, and impart to us its significance. (*Handing her the Star.*)

ADAH—My duty is to point hopefully to the blue expanse, beyond which lie the happy homes of our departed. (*Draws the Blue flower from the Floral Star, and holding it up, returns the star to the Patron, saying:*) This Blue flower, symbolizing Friendship, teaches the lesson of Undying Love. In the belief that true love is undying, I deposit this memento of our love in the grave with the remains of our departed Sister. (*Drops the flower into the grave.*)

BURIAL SERVICE

PATRON—Sister Ruth, select that portion of the Floral Star which suggests your particular duty, and impart to us its significance. (*Handing her the Star.*)

RUTH—My duty is to point to the golden tints of sunset, emblematical of the peaceful death-bed of those who sweetly sleep in the Lord. (*Draws the Yellow flower from the Floral Star, and, holding it up, returns the star to the Patron, saying:*) This Yellow flower, symbolizing disinterested Kindness, teaches the lesson of Unending Possession. We believe that it is only that which we have given in the true spirit of Charity that abides with us when earthly treasures pass away. Believing this, we lay our beloved ones in the grave, trusting them to the hands of Him Who will never forfeit the guardianship of our jewels. In the belief that true love is unending, I deposit this memento of our remembrance in the grave of our departed Sister. (*Drops the flower into the grave.*)

PATRON—Sister Esther, select that portion of the Floral Star which suggests your particular duty, and impart to us its significance. (*Handing her the Star.*)

ESTHER—My duty is to point to the pure robes of the saints, as indicative of the spotless inheritance reserved for those who live in the faith of the one ever-living God. (*Draws the White flower from the Floral Star, and, holding it up, returns the Star to the Patron saying:*) This White flower, symbolizing Truth and Innocence, teaches the lesson of Heart Purity. A promise of ineffable consolation was once made, admist the lilies on the mountain-side, "Blessed are the pure in heart, for they shall see God!" Believing this, the humble may look up—the lowly may hope, for the Unerring Eye will detect them amidst the flowers of His field, and they shall not fail to realize His promise: "Come, ye blessed of my Father, inherit the kingdom!" In the belief that no word of God can be lost, I deposit this emblem of our reverence for the will of God in the grave. (*Drops flower into the grave.*)

PATRON—Sister Martha, select that portion of the Floral Star which suggests your duty, and impart to us its significance. (*Handing her the Star.*)

MARTHA—My duty is to point to the verdure of God's evergreen trees as a symbol of the unfading glories of the heavenly groves. (*Draws the Green sprig from the Floral Star, and, holding it up, returns the Star to the Patron, saying:*) This Evergreen, symbolizing Immortality, teaches the lesson of Undeviating Sincerity. They whose souls have been touched with celestial fire can know no change. Coldness may wound them, but they cannot be alienated. Absence only increases their devotion to Him who has won their hearts by His divine favor. As from the grave, ofttimes, the sweetest floweret springs, so from the anguish of death are born the richest proofs of undeviating sincerity. In the belief that true love is ever sincere, and, as an emblem of our faith in a blessed immortality, I deposit this emblem of our hope in the grave. (*Drops the sprig into the grave.*)

PATRON—Sister Electa, select that portion of the Star which suggests your particular duty, and impart to us its significance. (*Hands her the Star.*)

ELECTA—My duty is to point to the rosy tints of a brilliant sunrise, as promising a blissful resurrection to those who die in the Lord. (*Draws the Red flower from the Floral Star, and, holding it up, returns the Star to the Patron, saying:*) This Red flower, symbolizing Fervency, teaches the lesson of unfading Beauty. On the banks of the pure river of the water of life, clear as crystal, is the tree of life which yieldeth its fruit. There is no night there, neither sun nor moon; for the glory of God doth lighten all the blissful place. In the belief that sincere friendship is eternally beautiful, I deposit this memento of our affectionate remembrance with the body of our lamented Sister. (*Drops the flower into the grave.*)

MATRON—(*Steps forward and says:*) It is a natural wish that flowers should spring from the graves of those we love. In Paradise, we believe, they never wither. God has given us manifold and wondrous truths in the stars of heaven; but the revelation of His love is not less plain in the flowers that are the stars of earth.

Emblems of our own great resurrection,
Emblems of the brighter, better land.

We strew them over the body of our departed friend (*strewing flowers*), as an apt manifestation of our affection, equally of hope and of reliance on that beneficence of which they are the eloquent impersonation. (*Holding up a pure white rose, says:*)

This white rose, the queen of flowers, the perfection of beauty and fragrance is, from its spotless purity, a symbol of our belief that there is a purer and better state of existence beyond the grave. The pall may spread its velvet folds, and the sable plumes bow in stately gloom over the dead, but a single white rose, drooping amid its verdant foliage, speaks of our reliance on the Divine promise that we shall be like a watered garden, when the bodies of those who sleep in the Lord shall come forth from the grave, radiant in the transfiguration of evangelic luster. Lord of all power and might! all Thy works do praise Thee. We give thanks unto Thee for Thy great love, and do commend the spirit of our departed Sister to Thy keeping; that in the final judgment she may stand before Thee in glory. (*Drops the flower into the grave, saying:*)

Until then, beloved, rest in peace!

PATRON—How instructive are these lessons! Love undying and unending, animating hearts that are pure and sincere will inherit the unfading beauty of which the Holy Spirit hath spoken. In this belief, I deposit what remains of the Floral Star in the grave of our deceased Sister. (*Deposits the balance of the Floral Star in the grave.*) The duty we owe to the dead is performed. It remains that we who are living should so live and, by our actions, attend the coming of the day of fate, that we may neither be surprised nor leave our duties imperfect, nor our sins uncanceled, nor God unappeased; but that when our bodies, in their turn, descend to their graves, our souls may ascend to the regions of eternal light. Whatever fate is to befall us in this world, let the motto of our lives be: For the past, Charity; for the present Hope; and for the future Faith.

Soft and safe, my departed Sister, be this thine earthly bed! Bright and glorious be thy rising from it! Abundant and full of delightful perfume be the wild flowers that here shall flourish. May the earliest buds of spring unfold their beauties over this thy resting-place, and here may the sweetness of the summer's last rose linger longest. Though the cold blasts of autumn may lay them in the dust, and for a time destroy the loveliness of their existence, yet the destruction is not final, and in the spring-time they shall surely bloom again. So, in the bright morning of the world's resurrection, thy mortal frame, now laid in the dust by the chilling blasts of Death, shall spring again into newness of life, and expand in immortal beauty, in realms beyond the skies. Until then, dear Sister, until then, farewell!

A Benediction may be pronounced by the acting Clergy or the following Prayer, by the Chaplain or Associate Matron, or other person:

PRAYER

Almighty and merciful God, infinite in wisdom and goodness, extend to us the riches of Thy everlasting favor. Make us grateful for the benefits we enjoy, and crown us with immortal life and honor. Thou hast decreed that we all shall die and come to dust. Thou hast also decreed that we shall rise from death to everlasting life. In that faith may we live, ever remembering that here we have no abiding-place. In that faith may we die, ever believing that when our earthly house is dissolved, we shall be welcomed to that glorious mansion, not made with hands, eternal in the heavens. Aid these mourning friends to feel that the ties of kindred, affection, and friendship are not broken by death, and that the family in heaven and on earth are the same. Forgive our transgressions, strengthen us to perform our duties, comfort us in our sorrows, and take us at last unto Thyself in heaven. Amen.

Response by the members.
Amen and Amen.

ADDENDA

THE PENTAGRAM

By J. W. Colville

Great interest attaches to the Order of the Eastern Star, not only because it enables widows, mothers, sisters, wives and daughters of Masons to become identified with and auxiliary to the main Masonic body, but also on account of the deep significance of its majestic emblem, one of the most honored and expressive of all ancient religious and fraternal symbols. The five-pointed star is often called the Star of Bethlehem and, aside from the time-honored tradition that, at the time of the birth of Jesus, a star guided the Magi to Palestine, there is a deep ethical and spiritual suggestiveness in this beautiful emblem which may be profitably considered from more than a single standpoint.

Five noble historic women are heroines in the Order of the Eastern Star and these five women represent five distinct types of character, each admirable and each quite different from the other four. The five points of the pentagram can easily be taken to represent, in a wider significance, the five races of Humanity. The number five owes its dignified position to the fact of there being five fingers or digits on each hand, and the human hand is a member that reveals the great superiority of man over animal. Some animals have four well developed fingers and a diminutive thumb, but only human beings possess the entire five digits well rounded out. Five points of Fellowship is a highly significant expression, and this honorable number contains a wealth of suggestive meaning which could only be unfolded by scholars unusually well versed in ancient and mystic lore.

To turn our attention specially to the five heroines, Adah, Ruth, Esther, Martha, Electa, is to contemplate not only five great historical characters, but five types of womanhood embodying sterling qualities which change not with the passing of ages.

ADAH, Jephthah's heroic daughter, is stationed at the first point of the Star: her color is blue, indicative of constant faith and unfaltering fidelity. This majestic type of character is one that all must admire on account of its uncompromising integrity, even though it be at the price of great self-sacrifice.

The biblical incident on which the character of Adah is built is one that breathes a spirit so widely removed from our modern thought that it seems necessary to clarify the narrative to some extent, or better, to spiritualize it so that we, from the feature of the actual slaying of Jephthah's daughter, may

(11) — *I have seen His Star in the East.*
(12) — What do you hear?
(13) — *I have come to worship Him.*
(14) — I have six signs, five passes, and two mottoes: one a general, the other a special motto; a word; and a grip.
(15) — Raise the hands as high as the waist; interlace the fingers of the right and left hands.
(16) — *We have seen His star in the East, and are come to worship Him.*
(17) — *Fairest among thousands, altogether lovely.*
(18) — The CABALISTIC WORD upon the block of the Star, which in an examination, should be alternated, I commencing with F-A-T-A-L. Each letter is the initial of a word which, together, make up the special motto of the degree: *Fairest among thousands, altogether lovely*. On examination, these letters, or the words they represent, are given alternately by the person and the examiner, the person being examined giving the first letter or word.
(19) — The GRAND HONOR SIGN is made by crossing the arms over the breast, the right arm over the left, the ends of the fingers resting on the shoulders, and making a graceful bow while dropping the hands to the sides.
(20) The GRIP is given in three motions.
1st — Take the right hand of the person opposite in the ordinary manner of shaking hands.
2nd — Move the thumb to the fleshy part of the hand, between the thumb and forefinger, and
3rd — Give a slight pressure.

(5) The SIGN OF ESTHER is made by three motions.
1st — Raise the right hand, palm downward, a little over the head, as if touching a crown on the head.
2nd — Extend the hand forward, palm down, on a level with the eyes, as if touching a scepter held by a person opposite.
3rd — Carry the hand to the left breast; drop to the side.
(6) The PASS — *What wilt thou?*
For explanation of the SIGN, etc., see Ritual pages 110-111.

(7) The SIGN OF MARTHA is made by three motions.
1st — Join the hands together at the tips of the thumbs and fingers, forming the figure of a triangle.
2nd — Raise the triangle thus formed directly above the eyes.
3rd — Raise the eyes, looking through the triangle; drop hands.
(8) The PASS — *Believest thou this?*
For explanation of the SIGN, etc., see Ritual pages 114-115.

(9) The SIGN OF ELECTA is made by three motions.
1st — Place the tips of the fingers of the right hand on the left shoulder.
2nd — Place the tips of the fingers of the left hand on the right shoulder, thus crossing the arms over the breast, the left arm over the right.
3rd — Cast the eyes upward; drop hands to the sides.
(10) The PASS — *Love one another.*
For explanation of the SIGN, etc., see Ritual, page 119.

hold firmly to its stalwart heroism while turning away to redeem her father's vow. If a man and his daughter really believed that God required, or would be pleased with, a human sacrifice, they would be conscientious in offering it and it would therefore be as highly meritous from their point of view, as it would have been for Abraham to slay Isaac, had not the Angel of the Lord revealed to that illustrious patriarch that such was not the will of Heaven.

Civilized fathers today do not believe that God requires that they slay their offspring to redeem their vows, but the sacredness of a pledge is inviolable, therefore, we need to use discretion in taking obligations upon ourselves. An oath regarded as binding is not lightly taken and nothing can be more stimulating to discretion and other imperative virtues than to contemplate the irrevocably binding nature of a vow. From the spiritual viewpoint, a sacrifice to God is a complete consecration, an entire sancification. Consequently Adah does not appear before us symbolically as a maiden whose blood is shed at her own bequest by her father's sword, but as a young woman whose loyalty to conviction and whose devotion to a noble cause is so great that she would prefer death to dishonor.

Adah's character is that of those who are completely fearless where moral principle is involved, who would deliberately choose martyrdom in preference to disloyalty, and in their death, as in their life, there is no concealment, no hiding behind a veil. Adah will not die with her face covered for in that way criminals are slain and her fame must be untarnished with suspicion as it travels down the ages to inspire, with courage, generations still unborn. Blue, true blue, is the color of the sky on a clear, bright, sunshiny day; to behold the blue ray, we must look upward, for on the heights of moral elevation, far beyond the ordinary, is true heroism alone displayed. The sword and veil which are Adah's emblems forcibly suggest willingness to die, if need be, in a righteous cause.

RUTH, whose color is yellow and whose emblem is the sheaf, denoting plenty, is one of the most delightful characters in Bible History. As David and Jonathan are so frequently brought forward to exemplify the highest type of friendship between Brothers, Ruth and Naomi stand for the same loyalty between Sisters, and there is indeed a pathos in the friendship of Ruth for her mother-in-law which is absolutely unique. It was to this sad and sorrowful elderly woman, not a bright young comrade of her own age, that Ruth devoted herself untiringly. The exquisite words which voice her complete devotion constitute one of our most touching sacred solos, "Entreat Me Not to Leave Thee," which is known and loved everywhere.

The character of Ruth is so modest and yet so brave that we find in her single personality a most remarkable embodiment of the sterner and the milder virtues in complete accord. Ruth stands for the purest type of religious sentiment, for she does all with the consciousness that the Will of God is being fulfilled in all her undertakings. Yellow always typifies enlightenment.

ESTHER, who occupies the third section of the Star, can only be typified by white, as she is the conquering queen who gains a royal victory over cruelty and despotism in every form. Esther's great beauty and extraordinary strength of character shine out on the historic page with a luster time cannot dim. There is much in her history, however, which must be taken spiritually rather than literally, if this glorious heroine is to be an incentive, which she can well become, to the women of today. Ancient stories are nearly all couched in warlike imagery and the scene of conquest is usually a battlefield. This is as much the case with Indian as with Hebrew traditions, for we find Krishna in the *Bhagavad Gita* counseling his disciple, Arjuna, to fight resolutely and continuously until a final victory is won. The moral lesson is not far to seek, for warfare must be interpreted allegorically, and true it is that without persistent triumphs over adversaries, no crown of glory can be gained.

Esther and Mordecai are on the side of liberty and justice; Haman is the upholder of slavery and oppression in its most cruel and revolting forms. "Right is might," said Abraham Lincoln, in direct opposition to "Might makes right," a falsehood so often promulgated. Esther's emblem, the crown and sceptre, denote majesty and grace. Annually, at the festival of Purim, Jews in all parts of the world recite the Book of Esther, and many are the quaint ceremonies connected with this hilarious feast, which is peculiarly dedicated to merriment and hospitality. Portions of the best food must be sent at Purim to the poor and needy, and no one enters into the spirit of rejoicing truly who does not in some measure relieve those who are distressed. Esther is the embodiment of the highest tactfulness, entirely free from all suspicion, cowardice or duplicity, she is a veritable queen of right diplomacy, bringing about, through the agency of her acute womanly instinct, that which might never have been achieved by the regular and more obvious methods employed by those lacking the keen penetration essential to success in trying situations.

MARTHA, whose color is green, is brought forward as witness to faith in the soul's immortality. The Gospel story of Martha, Mary and Lazarus, supplies the foundation for this character who is associated with the evergreen and with the broken column, two widely different emblems typifying in the one case the uncertainty of all things temporal and, in the other, the immortality of all that is spiritual.

ELECTA, the fifth heroine, has red for her color, and the cup, an emblem of generosity, for her symbol. The story of Electa is that of a brave woman who, in a time of fierce persecution, offered an asylum of refuge to the falsely accused and the hunted; she is pictured as a wealthy and accomplished matron who lived in the days of St. John the Evangelist. Electa was renowned for her profuse benevolence to the needy and when she espoused the cause of Christianity, then in its infancy, she immediately became a stalwart champion of those who were persecuted by the Roman authorities on account of their unpopular faith. Making no distinction between the rich and the poor, she extended almost regal hospitality to the humblest members of the Christian flock, and by so doing exposed herself knowingly to reproach and danger. Persecution came to her as well as to the weak and the obscure, and she was eventually visited by a band of Roman soldiers who were commissioned to command her to deny her faith and insult its emblem. She fearlessly refused to recant, even though such a refusal cost her and her family a year in prison. At the expiration of that painful year a judge, who had often partaken of her hospitality, urged her to recant that her life might be spared, for, so rife had persecution become, all those who persisted in loyalty to the Christian faith were doomed to a cruel death.

Electa accepted martyrdom and died heroically, for no threat of torture could induce her to betray her faith. She passed from earth with the words of the Master on her lips: "Father, forgive them; they know not what they do," and thus achieved a martyr's victory. Red is always consecrated to those who have died willingly for what they have felt to be the truth and also to those who have shown the same disposition even though not called to endure the actual destruction of their flesh. The lesson taught by Electa is one of hospitality and bravery combined, a lesson as much needed today as at any period in the past.

In these five illustrious heroines we find portrayed five distinct types of character blending into a perfect unity like the five points of the immortal pentagram, one of the most sublime emblems employed in ancient and modern times.

THE STAR

Where the bright acacia waving
    Tells of life forever green,
Lo, yon starry-pointed graving
    The emblem of Faith is seen.

Star that gleamed in heavenly story,
    Oh, whisper tender hope in every ray,
Shine with the light of perfect glory,
    And lead to eternal day.

Lo, that star that went before them,
    Stood above the gentle guest!
Oh, for the mighty faith that bore them
    So far in the holy quest!

Guide us up among the mountains,
    Where true Adah smiled at death;
Lead us down beside the fountains,
    By the scene of Ruth's great faith.

Land of Persia s queen immortal,
    Star of matchless wonder, show;
Thence with Martha to the portal,
    As a guide to our glad feet go.

Where the rose of Sharon bloometh,
    By the martyr's grave afar,
There in mighty glory cometh
    So gently the Eastern Star.

Chapter Banner

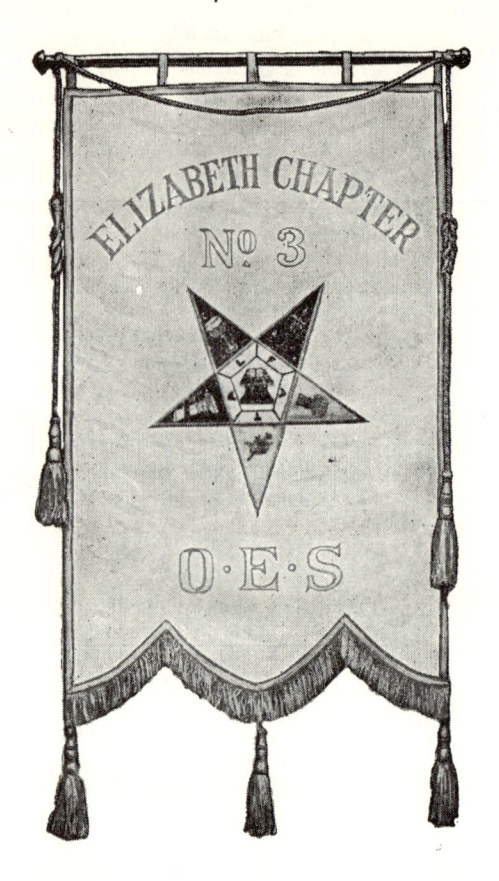

Eastern Star Signet